T0077946

CONFESSIONS
OF A
CHRISTIAN CYNIC

How I Found Meaning and Faith

Rev. Curt McCormack

BALBOA.PRESS
A DIVISION OF HAY HOUSE

Balboa Press books may be ordered through booksellers or by contacting:

Balboa Press
A Division of Hay House
1663 Liberty Drive
Bloomington, IN 47403
www.balboapress.com
844-682-1282

Cover Artwork by Musimack Marketing

Print information available on the last page.

ISBN: 978-1-9822-7118-3 (sc)
ISBN: 978-1-9822-7119-0 (e)

Balboa Press rev. date: 07/22/2021

REVIEWS

McCormack is trying to "redefine God for the 21st Century person". He has a two-fold audience in mind: 1. "Recovering Christians". 2. Millennials who are asking spiritual questions but do not align themselves with religious institutions, such as churches. For these two groups, I strongly recommend McCormack's passionate, clear, autobiographical, illuminating, at times humorous, series of essays.

---Dr. Bill Malcomson, Retired Dean and Seminary Professor

Curt and I have been discussing religion and all the areas it influences for nearly the last decade. I was raised Catholic and became a Baha'i in my mid-twenties. He was raised Evangelical and ordained a Baptist minister. We mostly share a common view with respect to the critical need for the populations of the world to embrace the underlying unity of God and His Messengers. His spiritual journey has taken him beyond the dogma and ritual of the currently limited orthodoxies of Christianity and he now embraces a more inclusive faith relevant for the 21st century.

---Dr. Allen McKiel, Retired Dean of Library Services, Western Oregon University

CONTENTS

EPIGRAPH

As such, those who understood that Jesus's teachings were meant to be about empowerment and self-love saw the threat to their own delusional power, and so they executed him. And when it was clear that this act only created a stronger force behind the lessons, they created religious dogma that skewed the teachings and made it seem to be advocating fear, judgment, and threats to the soul if one's behavior did not meet certain standards.

At the heart of every religion, just as at the heart of everything, from the smallest atomic speck of energy to the universe, lies the energy of love. And anything that induces fear is not centered in this Love and cannot be the truth.

Mike Dooley
Deep Space with Love

ACKNOWLEDGEMENTS

If I let my ego have its way, I would claim the following essays as my own. However, I don't live on an island but in a supportive community that encourages me to be all I can be and always work to serve the greater good. Therefore, it behooves me to extend a courteous 'Thank You' to some special folks who helped see this project through.

To my wife Jane, of 55 years, who oversees the grammatical structure of my writing along with understanding the content; if she doesn't understand it, most likely no one will.

To my sister, Robin Pelton, who gives me space and a place to write with an accompanying cup of coffee. She also proofread the text, making necessary corrections and questioned my intent with words that sometimes fill up a paragraph but says nothing.

To my friend and colleague, Dr. Bill Malcomson, seminary professor, who continues, even at 89, to be a mentor on my faith journey. Our continued conversations inspire and reflect a mind that still thinks deeply on spiritual things.

To Dr. Allen McKiel, retired Dean of Library Services at Western Oregon University, who, through his Baha'i perspective, challenges me to think outside the box, and who, at our weekly zoom meetings, helped clarify the content and intention of the manuscript.

To Margaret Anderson, a dear friend since seminary, who provided another eye on the proofreading.

To my daughter Stacey, Musimack Marketing, for prepping the mock-up for the cover and final draft, and her sister, Kerri, who continues to raise the "proud bar" as they serve the greater good through their work and life experience.

To my grandsons, Dylan and Wyatt, who make me laugh and offer a simple joy in their presence.

To all my Facebook friends who offer kind words on my postings.

…and to all of you who find a renewed purpose on your faith journey via my words.

PREFACE

"God is not a Christian; God is not a Jew, or a
Muslim, or a Hindu, or a Buddhist. All of those
are human systems that human beings have created
to try to help us walk into the mystery of God. I
honor my tradition. I walk through my tradition,
but I don't think my tradition defines God. I think
it only points me to God." - *John Shelby Spong*

My Journey as a Christian Cynic…
Ah, the cynic, the one who stands to the side or
back of the room and often sneers at people's motives
for being selfish or stupid. I am not sure that I am
a true cynic in that regard, but certainly, over the
years, my intolerance to be tolerant of extreme right-
wing conservatives and the 'Evangelical Literalist' or
fundamentalist has caused great discomfort to my soul.
I grew up in that evangelical environment, and only by
the Grace of God have I evolved from that belief to a
more inclusive and metaphorical belief in, what I would
call, Christ Consciousness.

Any worthy student of the history of Christianity

would understand the fundamentalist movement in the late 19th and early 20th century to be a strong reaction to the scientific community and its so-called anti-Biblical effect on the religious culture of that time. It was getting back to the "fundamentals" of the faith explicit in first-century Christianity, though that too, is a misnomer.

Theologian, Stephen D. Morris, speaking on behalf of Paul Tillich says:

> "Fundamentalism, especially in America, is a serious problem for Christianity. It is a way of thinking, more than anything else, which holds to strict black and white, either/or dogmas. For a fundamentalist, questions are not welcome, or maybe it's better to say, questioning the "fundamentals" is not welcome, no matter how logical or factually based those questions are. It depends on who you ask what these "fundamentals" are actually, but the classic ones for Christianity tend to include biblical inerrancy, a literal seven-day creation, penal substitutionary atonement, and, especially in modern times, homosexuality as a sin."

The sacred scriptures of the many faiths claim that they were written by God's revelation to a specific messenger. Even the act of revelation has its human thumbprint in the context of interpretation. The human presence in interpretation adds the dimension of time and culture sensitivity, language barriers, and the psychological make-up of the interpreter in what he/she thinks they hear and see. Conceptual truth is relative to the hearer and the seer. Though cynical as it sometimes is, it has been my journey to discover the Oneness of Spirit that exists in ALL the many faiths. If you were to strip all the religions of the world to their core beliefs, other than their cultural influences, you couldn't tell them apart. We all share the same "DNA" of creation; there is only one race, the human race; since there is great variety and color in God's creation of the human race, there are many paths to God. I have had the extreme joy of breaking bread with the Baha'i's and Hindus, prayed and meditated with the Muslims, Buddhists, and Jews, as well as those in my own faith tradition. I have felt welcomed, affirmed, and blessed by these traditions.

Please, understand that this journey is not about criticizing the Christian faith per se, but more specifically criticizing the fundamental issues of the church for its misrepresentation of the teachings of the Biblical narrative of both testaments. I have had to become a student of the history of Religions, more specifically of Christianity, to understand some of the subtle truths about the evolution of the Christian faith over the last 2000 years and its vital message of hope. I still claim the moniker of a Christian as that is my heritage, and I still believe very strongly in the teachings of Master Jesus. However, I could also be a Buddhist or Baha'i. This writing is about salvaging the "Christian" for the 21st century. Have I figured it out, and do I have all the answers? Nope! However, I have come to a place within my soul that I am on the right track.

This writing is about my personal journey toward enlightenment. This is my journey, and I expect no one to follow me or believe like me. This is my journey, not yours. If, by some chance, my journey inspires you to find your own path, then my work has been worthy of the effort.

What I am about to say is not new. It has been said by others—the early reformers from Huss to Luther in 14th and 15th century, who were very much concerned about the corruption of the faith by the ecclesiologists of the time. Most recently, Bishop John Shelby Spong envisions a New Christianity for a New World. According to Spong, a new world of Christianity can only happen if the fundamentals of the faith are challenged and revisited through the eyes of a 21st century Christian.

Spong argues that no one would want to be treated by a doctor that only used 18th-century medicine, let alone by a doctor from the first century. Regardless of our religious persuasion (Religious Science excluded), most of us would want to be treated with the most recent medical advances, including drugs. How many of us would give up our computers and go back to pad and pen? Who would trade their microwave for an open campfire? Who would willingly trade their washer and dryer for the washboard and tub? Who would give up their smart phones, pagers? And, of course, the list goes on! Most of us worship at the feet of technology because it makes our life more convenient but doesn't always lead us on our spiritual path.

I remember the first time I went to the library to look up a book, and I couldn't find the card catalog. I asked at the desk, and they said it was gone, replaced by the computer, which was very user-friendly. I was not going to be bullied by technology; I wanted the card catalog, which was familiar and user-friendly to me. Needless to say, I left the library without my book, unwilling to deal with technology. It was some months later before I went back, and I knew I would eventually have to confront the computer demon and learn how to navigate the computer if I ever wanted to find my book. I did go back, and the computer has since become my friend. Granted, we still have disagreements now and then, but we are managing just fine.

The point is, we welcome technology and the vast explosion of new ideas into all areas of our lives but one—religion. We still worship and pay homage to a dogmatic interpretation of scriptures derived from a certain time period in history with a very time-sensitive and cultural understanding. Does not God's message to God's people roll and change with the times?

We can certainly see a shift in the evolution of who God is from the Old to the New Testament. Traditionalists play the "Jesus Christ the same yesterday and today" card, which has nothing to do with anything except the fact that God's love, exemplified in Jesus, is a constant. "As it was in the beginning, is now and ever shall be." Yet how we experience that love and wrestle with the ethical and moral issues of that love in the 21st Century is not only timely but essential.

A 2018 article posted on Facebook by writer and speaker Sam Eaton claims that *59 Percent of Millennials Raised in a Church Have Dropped Out—*" According to this study (and many others like it), church attendance and impressions of the church as well as peoples leaving the church, are the lowest in recent history, and most drastic among millennials described as 22- to 35-year-olds.

- Only 2 in 10 Americans under 30 believe attending a church is important or worthwhile (an all-time low).
- 59 percent of millennials raised in a church have dropped out.

- 35 percent of millennials have an anti-church stance, believing the church does more harm than good.
- Millennials are the least likely age group of anyone to attend church (by far). As I sat in our large church's annual meeting last month, I looked around for anyone in my age bracket. It was a little like a Titanic search party..."

Megachurch Evangelical pastor Jim Palmer of Brentwood, TN, walked out of his church because the "old, old story" wasn't meeting the needs of the people he served. He says, "Beneath the appearance and the surfaces of people's lives, there was a level of suffering and brokenness for which my theology did not touch." In an April 2021 column in the Miami Herald titled, "Small Wonder that the Church is Shrinking." Leonard Pitt's Jr. says, "For the first time since Gallup began tracking religious membership back in 1937, it has dropped below half. Back then, 73 percent of us belonged to some house of worship. Today, just 48 percent do." Pitts further states that despite the decline of church membership, according to Gallup, 87 percent of Americans still believe in God.

This goes to my point that the Christian experience has failed to meet the needs of its members and needs a 21st-century revival. Bishop Spong has a name for all the folks that have left the church and no longer find traditional Christianity viable in their life. He calls them "The Church Alumni Association." They have left the church but have not necessarily given up on Christianity. There but for the Love of God go I. These are some of the people my essays are written to reach.

Like Spong, I agree, if Christianity is to survive, it must change and find meaning and expression in the 21st century. The essays that follow are my attempt to offer some gentle nudges in that direction. They are not scholarly dissertations, as I am not a scholar in the academic sense. They are conclusions I have made over the last fifty years of pastoral ministry, philosophical studies, and Biblical scholarship through reading and personal study. I understand that I bring my own bias to these conclusions, and I will claim them as such. I am convinced that the God of Abraham, Isaac, and Jacob is very much alive but not in the way we have come to understand the Old and the New Testament scripture. I honestly believe God longs for a relationship with us, but the 21st-century Christian has a problem with a God that appears to be a fearful despot or a vengeful autocrat.

The following essays might well disturb some of you. I only ask that you read them with an open mind and heart, and maybe like me, you will be touched by a living Spirit that will lead you on a journey you can't, even yet, imagine!

I bid you blessings on your journey…

Rev. Curt McCormack, 2021

CONFESSIONS OF A CHRISTIAN CYNIC

"There was a time when I had all the answers. My real growth began when I discovered that the questions to which I had the answers were not the important questions." - *Reinhold Niebuhr*

B eginning the Journey...
It was the first day of first grade, and the teacher asked us what we wanted to be when we grew up. Many of the usual answers were given, i.e., farmers, loggers, teachers, etc., a traditional answer given the culture of our rural Polk County life. When she got around to me, I blurted out, "I'm going to be a preacher!" I have not a clue why I said that.

It is true; I was somewhat fascinated with the lives of the many preachers and Evangelists that came through our small country church, especially the frustrated entertainers that dramatically preached their gospel with a lot of shouting and physicality.

I grew up in the rural part of the Willamette Valley

of Oregon in a small lumber/farming community called Pedee. It was one of those 'blink and miss it' kind of communities. There was a general store, service station/garage, café, two taverns, and a church, and of course, a four-room schoolhouse, 1 through 8th grade. Except for the schoolhouse and the church, none of the others are there now. I lived a mile or so south-west from this 'city center,' close to the four-room schoolhouse and the Evangelical United Brethren church.

It's true that it takes a village to raise a child, and I was definitely a product of that rural culture and mentality. Most of my neighbors growing up were aunts, uncles, and cousins. My parents were regular churchgoers, and I spent many a Sunday morning in Sunday school and summers in Vacation Bible School, sometimes Sunday night and Wednesday night as well. I learned a lot of memory verses and the morals of most of the basic Bible stories. My theology was handed down to me, a product of the conservative religious culture of this community. This contained alter calls, fearmongering of Hell, and the Devil was always out to get you.

As a child, I was given the story of the Bible, in excerpts and the basic principles of Christianity. God could not do his own work, so he sent his son, Jesus as a baby on Christmas, who grew up to preach and teach the "Good News." According to this narrative, the Jews did not like his teachings and had him crucified on a Roman cross where he died, was put in a cave-grave, and resurrected back to life on Easter Sunday. The theory being that his death was a sacrifice for all of humanity's sins. Consequently, if we ABC our life, that is, Ask for forgiveness, Believe "...on the Lord Jesus Christ," and Confess our sins...He, (God and also, sometimes Jesus as they are interchanged) "...is faithful and just to forgive us our sins and cleanse us from all unrighteousness." Can't believe I just pulled that out of the hat! Anyway, this action is called "accepting the Lord Jesus as our personal Savior and spending eternity with him." It means that we are saved from our past sins. Unfortunately, I don't believe that it carries forward. Theoretically, it would take many 'savings' over a lifetime. This was the core message. Any seeming contradictions or confusing facts were met with, "you must have faith and defeat doubt, don't let Satan in."

I 'sang this song' until I was a junior in college at Oregon State University. In all honesty, I don't know that I literally believed it, but it was a thumbprint on my life through those years. Looking back now, those years were important to my evolution and journey of faith.

I was extremely interested in religion, particularly Christianity, and took a lot of religion classes in college, many of which challenged my conservative position. Because my faith experiences up to now were inherited from my family and community, I reached a point where the "old, old story" did not make much sense to me. The writings of current theologians and philosophers opened a new world to me. I started with the fact that God is…I do not know what or who God is, but this would be my journey to find out.

In 1963, JAT Robinson, the then Bishop of Woolrich, published his classic book, "Honest to God." It was a critique on traditional theology and opened my eyes to a possible faith experience beyond the boundaries of the tradition that I had inherited. Biblical research was beginning to move outside the walls of historical expectation. Even Albert Schweitzer, with his 1910 English publication of The Historical Jesus, still an orthodox perspective, began to push some scholars to think and research outside the theological box.

I guess it was Paul Tillich, a philosopher and Lutheran theologian, who spoke to me in a way that made sense to my limited theological makeover. His term for God was "the ground of all being…". That made a lot of sense. I no longer thought of God anthropomorphically, that is, the white robe, long flowing beard, and deep voice, but thinking about God as the 'ground of all being' really resonated with me. God became the essence of all creation, the very core of all life, the "treeness of a tree," the "flowerness of a flower," the…. you get the picture!

Biblically, there are two statements that speak to the beingness of God—God is love (I John 4:8, NIV), and God is Spirit (2 Corinthians 3:17, NIV). I began to hang my understanding of God on these two verses. In my mind, they certainly confirmed that spirit and love are indeed the ground of all being.

By my senior year at OSU, I had made the decision to attend seminary and train to become a preacher/ pastor. I was not really sure what that meant, but it was something that came out of the core of my being. If you want to call it a "call to ministry," then so it was.

Because I had been infused in the Evangelical United Brethren Church (EUB), I was encouraged to attend the EUB seminary in Portland. This was a conservative nonaccredited seminary. I felt I needed to be somewhere else that would open me up to the reality of the culture at that time. So, in 1966, newly married, my wife and I headed off to seminary in Berkeley, California. Berkeley in the mid-'60s, what could possibly be wrong with that?

I had grown up in the Willamette Valley of Oregon, a very "wasppie" state at the time. There were very few blacks in some areas of Oregon as blacks were not allowed to stay overnight. The Klu Klux Klan was very active in this part of the Willamette Valley. There were a few Asians and some Latinos at OSU, but they were few and far between. Latinos were around during the summer to basically harvest the crops. At Oregon State, the only blacks on campus were football players, and at that time, they were few. There was a small Asian community, but most of the students were white Anglo-Saxon Catholics/ protestants. There were certainly no black professors, at least in the liberal arts school, that I recall. So, imagine my introduction to Berkeley in 1966. It was, indeed, overwhelming but also energizing in a positive 'Oh My God' what have I gotten myself into?

I had chosen to attend Berkeley Baptist Divinity School (later became American Baptist Seminary of the West), which was located on the south side of the University of California, a block and a half from "People's Park" and two blocks from Telegraph Avenue, which was the radical heart of the student unrest which ended at UC Berkeley's Sproul Plaza. On the north side of the UC Berkeley campus was Holy Hill which housed several other seminaries, Lutheran, Episcopal, Methodist/ Congregational, Unitarian, Jesuit, and others, plus the Graduate Theological Union, which was the beginning of a shared graduate program bringing together all the seminaries for a common core program. My class was part of this first-year experiment. We had common core lectures at other seminaries, and each denomination ran their own indoctrination program back at their home campus.

Because of the GTU, I was able to experience some of the best theologians and historical professors of the day. Though I was a mediocre student at best, I loved my time at BBDS. I need to say that Berkeley Baptist, by its implied name, was part of the American Baptist tradition. I knew nothing about Baptists, especially being EUB. However, there was a clue in my junior year at OSU while taking a class on the Sermon on the

Mount with Dr. Warren C. Hoveland. We were to write a paper on our conclusions on the study of this particular sermon. Dr. Hoveland's comment took me back a bit. He wrote, "A very traditional Baptist understanding." What's that you say, a Baptist understanding? I had no idea what that meant; I didn't even know any Baptists, let alone what Baptist Theology was. So, evidently, the seed had been sown.

Toward the end of my Junior year in Seminary, Berkeley Baptist Divinity School became American Baptist Seminary of the West. There were essentially two ABC seminaries on the west coast, BBDS in Berkeley and California Theological Seminary in Covina. The restructuring gave a new name, hence the American Baptist Seminary of the West with two campuses. There were all kinds of reasons for the merger, but funding proved to be the bottom line. Merging the two seminaries would save a lot of dollars from shrinking church and private donations that supported the seminaries. From a student perspective, the two seminaries were still exclusively unique to their base, Covina's being very conservative and Berkeley's being liberal. Six years after this name change, the Covina faculty was relocated to Berkeley.

During my middle (second year) year, ABSW got a new professor of preaching and field education by the name of Dr. William (Bill) Malcomson. Dr. Bill was a marvelous professor. He took teaching very seriously and students as well. He was a critical thinker and passed that on to his students. I really enjoyed Bill's classes. It was like he was a student with us, engaged us in discussion/conversation, never presumed that he had all the answers but searched with us so that our discovery was intentional and self-affirming. Bill became my mentor and continues to be a friend and colleague for some 50 years hence.

As a Middler (2nd year), I developed a passion for creative worship services, or as it was tagged then, 'contemporary worship.' I was encouraged by the results of Vatican II that produced the folk masses of the 60s/70s. A lot of Christian folk songs and contemporary hymns were written during this period. As a musician, I was also writing my own songs for worship. As my middler year ended, I was offered an internship for the next school year to move to a community north of Seattle and pastor a church while the regular pastor went on sabbatical. By this time, I was finding my way into the American Baptist tradition and feeling comfortable with its polity and theology. Good Shepherd Baptist Church in Lynnwood, WA, proved to be a veritable laboratory of learning for me and truly whetted my appetite for pastoral ministry. I was a good and strong worship leader but a mediocre preacher at best, with good people skills that allowed me to get along with almost anybody.

The Lynnwood church was a good and vital church— small but people engaged in mission and ministry, a credit to Bernie Turner, the regular pastor. I think I experienced every aspect of pastoral ministry that can happen in the life of a church and pastor. There were weddings, funerals, broken relationships, depression, spiritual disconnection, and my lack of experience with all of these. However, it did cement my call to pastoral ministry.

When I came back to seminary for my senior year, I knew what I wanted to do.

In order to succeed at the pastoral ministry, there were some specific classes I needed to take to gain some knowledge and language about specific aspects of ministry.

I needed some counseling classes. Also, I wanted to increase my experience with contemporary worship, but alas, there were none offered. To the rescue was Bill Malcomson, who said, "Let's see if we can make one happen." He did. This was a whole new field of worship and ritual, so there were no boundaries to tie us to tradition. This class really helped me think through the elements of traditional worship and how contemporary worship might revitalize some of those elements.

In my mind, mainline protestant worship culture had become dull, boring, and predictable. Should the Holy Spirit want to visit any congregation, she/he would have had a hard time getting the people's attention. I'm reminded of a story that illustrates this point. A homeless, disheveled man was walking by a church one

Sunday evening and was drawn in by the music. He marched himself down to the front row and sat quietly for a few minutes when an usher came and asked him to leave because he wasn't dressed appropriately. He left the sanctuary and sat sadly on the front steps. As he sat, he heard a voice saying, "I'm sorry, my son, but I have been trying to get into that congregation for years!"

If I recall, there was only one African American student in my seminary class. I think he came in my middler year. He was extremely well-spoken and was already pastoring a black congregation. I have to confess; I had an affinity for the African American church. Most have a very informal ritual and liturgy, a lot of music, a sense of openness, freedom of expression, and are not consumed by the clock or future need to get folks home for the football game. Their worship is very "subjective" in nature, as are many of the Pentecostal churches. One of my aunts and uncles on my mom's side were Assembly of God members, and I can remember attending church with them, hearing them speaking in tongues and the "moving of the Holy Spirit" as it was called. This style of worship doesn't rely on a printed menu to assure the worship leaders stay on task. It fosters spontaneity.

Mainline Protestantism was addicted to the 'order of worship' so the congregants could see by the order how long they would have to sit uncomfortably to be preached at before they could go home. I'm being overly facetious. Their ritual (what they do) was predictable, basically the same format every Sunday. Their liturgy (how they do it) was also predictable, leaving little or no room for spontaneity. True, the music was particularly good but also predictable.

I guess I would sum up the two worship styles as 'subjective worship' and 'objective worship.' Mainline Protestantism uses an objective format for worship.

That is, they experience God through tradition, the Bible, theology, creeds, prayer, and the body of the church. There is nothing wrong with that, in and of itself, but my experience is that God is not predictable, and to confine him/her to an ordered ritual, in my mind, defeats the purpose of worship.

African American and Pentecostal worship is more 'subjective in nature, experiencing God through feelings, emotions, and even ecstasy. Yes, they also include the Bible and prayer. Neither of these styles are 'wrong' or 'right' in and of themselves.

My interest in 'contemporary worship' was primarily to bring more subjectivity to the objective format of mainline Protestantism. How do you plan for spontaneity? How do you allow for God to move in and among the objective elements of worship? On the one hand, it's trying to put new wine in old wineskins…as scripture attests, and that's never a good idea. On the other, it is trying to become "new wine" by creating a new wineskin, and yes, good luck with that!

Sometime in the mid-'70s, I created the Center for

Contemporary Worship. This was my attempt to help congregations to move beyond traditional worship. I had all kinds of printed resources and offered workshops to experience some of the new elements of what was 'contemporary worship.' During that period, I produced a songbook and worship manual called "Gonna Shout for Joy, new ventures in worship and song." A fellow colleague, who had a press in his home, printed the book. Another friend and colleague wrote the lead sheets for the music. An artist friend did the artwork. I marketed it through various religious magazines and word of mouth. The Center was active for about five years. I still strongly believed in the notion of creative worship, but my own personal journey has moved me beyond the hallowed walls of traditional Christianity.

I've always been an 'armchair' scholar of the Bible, interested in the changing theology and historical reference of the Biblical record. Theology and Christology were moving beyond the sacred walls of what had been traditional Christianity. Thanks to the theologians and scholars of the Jesus Seminar, Robert Funk, John Crossan, Marcus Borg, Bart Ehrman, JS Spong, and a volley of others, the notion of Jesus, as the son of God, his divinity, and the impact of his teachings were being critically and historically revisited, unveiling what it means for 21st-century Christians. I was particularly drawn to Bishop John Shelby Spong, who claimed that the long-standing tradition of Christianity was no longer viable for the 21st century. He was a prolific writer on the subject and proposed a new vision for Christianity based on modern Biblical research and the metaphorical meaning of the scriptures.

Yet it was not until I read the Autobiography of a Yogi by Paramahansa Yogananda.*

Did I really understand the teachings of Jesus? The following piece from his work on Jesus explains the spiritual connection:

> "The lack of individual prayer and communion with God has divorced modern Christians and Christian sects from Jesus' teaching of the real perception of God, as is true also of all religious paths inaugurated by God-sent prophets whose followers drift into byways of dogma and ritual rather than actual God-communion. Those paths that have no esoteric soul-lifting training busy themselves with dogma and building walls to exclude people with different ideas. Divine persons who really perceive God include everybody within the path of their love, not in the concept of an eclectic congregation but in respectful divine friendship toward all true lovers of God and the saints of all religions." (excerpted from" The Second

Coming of Christ," published by the Self Realization Fellowship sometime in the mid to late 1920s.)

I was struck by the sentence, *"The lack of individual prayer and communion with God has divorced modern Christians and Christian sects from Jesus' teaching of the real perception of God…"* I'm also reminded of the words of Gandhi, *"I like your Christ, but I do not like your Christians, they are so unlike your Christ."*

My distress with the mainline Christian Church has to do with the fact that dogma and ritual have been more important than the teachings of Jesus. Jesus, like the Buddha, taught loving kindness. The beatitudes (Attitudes for being) and the Sermon on the Mount found in the Gospel of Matthew are the core teachings of Jesus, the Christ. The Apostle Paul helped develop the core teachings of the early church, in essence, about living the Mind of Christ.

To many, so-called Christian Churches today teach hate, hate from the perspective that God hates gays, God hates abortions, God hates left-handers, God hates…go ahead, fill in the blanks. An interesting point here is the fact that they can have a God, supposedly of Love that hates…it makes absolutely no sense! God is either a God of love, or God is not.

The context for me was spiritual experience over belief in dogma and ritual. I am not saying that you cannot find the God experience through dogma and ritual, only that I could not. Paramahansa brought home to me the notion that all spiritual teachings, regardless of the teacher, speak to the core of spirit and share the same message that "all humanity shares the same DNA; we are one in Spirit, one in Love, one race, one humanity. You will find the teaching of **the Golden Rule in almost all religious traditions—at the very core, we are the same. One God, many paths.

Even by calling God, God, we are limiting the very nature of God. One of the monikers used by Judaism is Yahweh which literally means the no-name God, or as Exodus 3:14, NIV states, (Yahweh) I AM, THAT I AM. To give God a name is to limit God.

Using the term God also renders an anthropomorphic concept of a human-like person in a white robe and long flowing beard. John 4:24 tells us that "God is spirit and we must worship (him) in spirit and truth." By referring to God as spirit takes away the notion of an anthropomorphic type of God. As I mentioned earlier, I liked Paul Tillich's phrase for God, "the ground of being" the soul of the universe. God as spirit speaks to me, also God as energy, the energy of the universe that gives life to all living. We all have to reconcile who and what we determine God to be. It is from that understanding that we find our place in the universe.

If you were to ask me today what kind of religious label I would consider myself, I would have to say Heinz

57! However, in saying that, I still have a strong foothold in the teachings of Jesus, with which I have wrestled and honored all my life to date. I have a great affinity for the Bahai' faith, historical Judaism and have planted some seeds in Buddhism. Some time ago, I was sharing with a friend the nature of my faith journey, saying that I have an affinity for many faith traditions but would probably not be 'good' in any of them. She replied, "Yes, but you are a good Curt!" And, to that end, I shall continue to strive.

*Paramahansa Yogananda (born Mukunda Lal Ghosh; January 5, 1893 – March 7, 1952) was an Indian monk, yogi, and guru who introduced millions to the teachings of meditation and Kriya Yoga through his organization Self-Realization Fellowship (SRF) and Yogoda Satsanga Society (YSS) of India; he lived his last 32 years in America. A chief disciple of the Bengali yoga guru Swami Sri Yukteswar Giri, he was sent by his lineage to spread the teachings of yoga to the West, to prove the unity between Eastern and Western religions, and to preach a balance between Western material growth and Indian spirituality.[2] His long-standing influence in the American yoga movement, and especially the yoga culture of Los Angeles, led him to be considered by yoga experts as the "Father of Yoga in the West." (Wikipedia)

** THE GOLDEN RULE

CHRISTIANITY: Whatever men should do to you, do so to them. (Matthew 7:12, NIV)

JUDAISM: You shall love your neighbor as yourself. (Leviticus 19:18, NIV)

ISLAM: Not one of you is a believer until he loves for his brother what he loves for himself. (Forty Hadith)

JAINISM: A man should wander about treating all creatures as he himself would be treated. (Sutrakritanga)

CONFUCIANISM: Try your best to treat others as you would wish to be treated yourself, and you will find that this is the shortest way to benevolence. (Mencius)

HINDUISM: One should not behave towards others in a way which is disagreeable to oneself. (Anusasana Parva)

BUDDHISM: Comparing oneself to others in such terms as "Just as I am So are they, just as they are so am I," he should neither kill nor cause others to kill. (Sutta Nipata)

A CASE FOR GOD

"The Christian life is not about pleasing God, the finger-shaker and judge. It is not about believing now or being good now for the sake of heaven later. It is about entering a relationship in the present that begins to change everything now. Spirituality is about this process: the opening of the heart to the God who is already here." - *Marcus Borg*

Let me begin this essay by saying that I am not arguing whether or not God exists; I assume that. What I am arguing is, what is the nature, character, and will of God for the 21st century?

A story is told of a five-year-old in a Sunday School class. The teacher had asked each of the students to draw and color a picture of something they liked about creation. The five-year-old was diligently at work when the teacher came by and inquired about his picture. "I'm drawing a picture of God," he said matter-of-factly. The teacher, rather surprised, exclaimed, "But we don't know what God looks like." Without hesitation, the five-year-old responds, "We will when I get through!"

Most likely, the drawing would involve a 'man' in a long white robe with a long white beard. It seems that Christianity has inspired that kind of image of God. This image, of course, transpires from a perspective of Biblical history that depicts a God who is quick to anger, jealous, resentful, and revengeful. It is as if we have created God in our own image rather than as scripture says, "God created humankind in God's own image." We have allowed God to become anthropomorphized. Bishop John Shelby Spong calls this notion of God "theism" and argues that this is *a "…human definition, not a divine revelation".* Spong continues, *"the theistic God in these various traditions (Islam, Judaism, and Christianity) was always other, always external to the self who was defining the God-figure, always supernatural, and, at least in the West, usually personal in the sense that individuals could know and communicate with this deity. The theistic God was also presumed to be the explanation for that which was beyond rational understanding, a being capable of miraculous power who therefore needed to be supplicated, praised, obeyed, and pleased."*

Consequently, we get a God that gets angry when he/she doesn't get his/her way, is jealous, and reaps revenge on all and everyone that does not conform to his/her eccentric will. Is it any wonder that Christians are becoming former Christians?

2

An article written some years back by Ann Graham (daughter of Billy Graham) responded to the question, "Why does God allow evil things to happen to Americans?" She responded in part by justifying God's absence with the assertion that we have kicked God out of our schools, our courtrooms, in some cases, even our churches, and, "...*God, being the perfect gentleman he is, has backed down.*" This is the very thing I am talking about. Notice that according to Graham, God is not only a 'He,' but a perfect gentleman...and he backs down! What kind of God would back down recoiling from his creation? Remember the flood, tower of Babel, Sodom, and Gomorrah? If God lives within each individual who proclaims that they have accepted him into their heart, God is within them 24/7 wherever they go: in the church, into court, in the school, under the apple tree. People who are filled with Spirit-Energy will take God with them into the court, into the school, and even the church.

Perhaps the problem is that some "Christians" can ONLY find God in their humongous, elaborate, expensive church because they have zero Spirit-Energy within themselves.

There are sources that suggest that this kind of a theistic God will most likely not survive the 21st century. Christianity is on the decline, and the theistic God concept is one of the most likely reasons.

Culturally, we have allowed science and technology

to improve our lives in all areas except our religion. For whatever reason, we cling to a God concept derived out of antiquity and refuse to let God come of age. Atheists have long denied the existence of a theistic God, and the religious society has scoffed and condemned them.

Neal Donald Walsh, author of the Conversation with God series, says it this way, *"there are five fallacies about God that create spiritual crisis, violence, killing and war, First, the idea that God needs something. Second, the idea that God can fail to get what God needs. Third, the idea that God has separated you from Him because you have not given Him what He wants. Fourth, the idea that God still needs what He needs so badly that God now requires you, from your separated position, to give it to Him. Fifth, the idea that God will destroy you if you do not meet His requirements."* (Neal Donald Walsh, What God Said, 2013, The Berkeley Group.)

This is what mainline Christianity has become and the reason for the continued decline of church membership. Megachurch Evangelical pastor, Jim Palmer of Brentwood, TN, walked out of his church because the "old, old story" wasn't meeting the needs of the people he served. He says, *"Beneath the appearance and the surfaces of people's lives, there was a level of suffering and brokenness for which my theology did not touch."* How do we redefine God for the 21st century Christian? The answer begs a voluminous number of words to cover all the bases, as it were. However, I shall attempt to do so in this short essay.

The universe is permeated with a "creative life force." It is Spirit-Energy that exists in ALL things, both animate and inanimate. That very Spirit-Energy is what makes a tree a tree, a flower a flower, a rock a rock. Physicists tell us that rocks are alive with subatomic particles. Though they move at a much slower rate, rocks are still filled with energy. The essence of all creation is this Spirit-Energy which, for lack of a better term, I call God. To try and put a description on this God is to limit God's possibilities. The ancient Jews understood this as they referred to God as 'Yahweh,' I AM, the no-name God. By giving God a name, you put limitations on who and what God is. Therefore, this Spirit-Energy "God" is infinite in ALL things. Human consciousness cannot comprehend infinity, much less the nature of God. God is all-Possessing and All-Knowing: also, infinite knowledge; God is infinite wisdom; God is infinite possibility; God is infinite compassion, mercy, and Love, ad infinitum. If God, therefore, is infinite in all things, then God must, likewise, be infinite in happiness. What is it then that we humans can do to make God happier? It seems to me that if God is infinite happiness, then there is nothing we humans can do to improve on that happiness.

From the back of the room comes a concerning voice, "God wants us to worship Him!" Ah yes, the very reason for every Sunday church service, or 'worship service' as it is often called.

What does it mean to worship?

The dictionary definition (among many) is "A *show of reverence and adoration for (a deity); honor with religious rites.*"

In Christianity, worship is the act of attributing reverent honor and homage to God. It will most likely involve singing endless praise songs, litanies, shouts of Amen! prayer, reading of scripture, preaching, sacred dance, organ, piano, and in some cases, a four-or five-piece band.

My point is that worship is of no consequence to God. God needs no feeding the ego like some presidents we have had. You don't need to do it; you can or not. If that is true, so why, then, worship? Good question. First, Worship is really more about appeasing us, the individual and the congregation than God. It seems that we need to prove our commitment and worthiness to God, and this is how we do it. Any guilt that comes when we do not do what we know to be true is not from God but from our misunderstanding of what we are doing.

Secondly, if God needs nothing from us, humans, what is the point? The point, I believe, is soul work, expressing our divinity. As Walsh says, *"...the only motivation that makes sense to our soul is the goal of experiencing, expressing, and demonstrating Divinity."* It is through soul work that

CONFESSIONS OF A CHRISTIAN CYNIC

we strive to be merciful, compassionate, and peacemakers. We are accountable for our own soul journey. There is no judgment from God regarding whether or not we succeed. We inherently know if we are, as St. Paul says, "...falling short of our mark."

Hmmm. But the Bible is full of scripture that encourages us to worship God, and not to do so is an abomination. To be sure, Old Testament scripture feeds that mentality. The OT God was understood as a theistic (anthropomorphic) God and needed constant praise and adoration. It is interesting that the New Testament has a different take on worshipping God. In the 4th chapter of John NIV, *Jesus says that "God is Spirit, and those that worship him must do so in Spirit and Truth."* God is Spirit, Soul-Energy if you please, not anthropomorphic looking, and acting like us. God is the "wind beneath our wings," so to speak. Any worship to be done needs to be done in "Spirit and in Truth." To worship in Spirit, remembering that worship is for us and not God, means that our words need to come from within—that's where we are told the Kingdom of God is. The 'within' is obviously from the heart. That is "Spirit" worship.

To worship in 'Truth.' What does that mean? What truth are we talking about? It would be the truth that God is spirit and desires that we walk daily in the fruits of that Spirit, "...love, joy, peace, patience, kindness, goodness, faithfulness, gentleness, and self-control. *(Galatians 5:24-25, NIV)* That is the truth of Jesus' teaching and what Walsh meant by 'demonstrating our divinity.' Paul confirms this in *Romans 12:1, NIV "Therefore, I urge you, brothers and sisters, in view of God's mercy, to offer your bodies as a living sacrifice, holy and pleasing to God—this is you true and proper worship."* What is the living sacrifice? Dedicating ourselves to the fruits of the Spirit. The simple answer would be Micah 6:8, NIV, *"What does the Lord require of you but to serve justice, love mercy and walk humbly with your God."* The Four Agreements, from author Don Miguel Ruis, offers helpful tools to work at Divinity for 21ˢᵗ century Christians: *Agreement 1: Be Impeccable With Your Word. Agreement 2: Don't Take Anything Personally. Agreement 3: Don't Make Assumptions. Agreement 4: Always Do Your Best.*

The Universe/Spirit Energy or God, trusts us, his/her children, to do the right thing. What is the right thing? That which resonates in our soul and encourages us to love and serve others with reckless abandon! If the voice asks you to harm or kill those who disagree with you, that is not the voice of God but the misfire of your brain.

I like what ND Walsh has to say about God, *"We are all part of God and cannot be separated from God. We are all also a part of each other and cannot be separated from each other."* Carl Sagen used to say that we are all made out of stardust. We all possess the same Divine DNA. We are all, regardless of birth origin, gender, skin color, and geography, spiritual brothers and sisters. Now and again, we will have some sibling rivalry, but hopefully not enough to destroy the family. Walsh says it another way, *"We are all One. All things are One Thing. There is only One Thing, and all things are part of the One Thing There Is. This means that we are Divine. We are not our body, we are not our mind, and are not our soul. We are the unique combination of all three, which compromises the totality of us. This is the Trinity. You are an individuation of Divinity, and an expression of God on Earth."*

The glue that binds all this together is, of course, Divine love. *I John NIV* confirms this in *chapter 4: verse 8*, God is love. The Spirit-Energy of creation is, indeed, Love. As I mentioned above, our task in this lifetime is to demonstrate our Divinity. We do that by serving others through justice, compassion, mercy, and peaceful resolve. These are steps taken toward recognizing the All-Possessing Spirit of God Within. When we put that kind of love in the hands of you and me, wonderful and blessed things happen! Mother Theresa reminds us that "helping hands are holier than praying lips."

I know old habits are hard to break, and convenience itself will warrant still talking about the Sunday morning service as a worship service. So, let it be. I still enjoy gathering with folks to sing and play the old hymns. Though I don't agree with a lot of the theology, I can still sing them with gusto and know that grace abounds. If you want to call that worship, do so; I will call it celebrating our Christian past. Doesn't matter what we call it; the results are the same. Blessings!

THE BIBLE AS THE INSPIRED, INERRANT AND LITERAL WORD OF GOD

"In the entire first Christian century, Jesus is not mentioned by a single Greek or Roman historian, religion scholar, politician, philosopher or poet. His name never occurs in a single inscription, and it is never found in a single piece of private correspondence. Zero! Zip references." – *Bart D. Ehrman*

"My point, once again, is not that those ancient people told literal stories and we are now smart enough to take them symbolically, but that they told them symbolically and we are now dumb enough to take them literally." – *John Dominic Crossan*

God did not write the Bible, neither did Jesus, and, most likely, neither did Moses. I do not believe that we can say that God even dictated the Bible. Whoever the Biblical writers were, they wrote out of a specific cultural context, a timeframe, and personal bias. They took the facts, as they understood them, from their community of faith and wrote them down accordingly.

Inspiration, by whatever means, happens contextually, that is, it is cultural, framed by a specific time period, and relegated to the idiosyncrasies of the writer. Whoever the author of Genesis was (scholarship indicates that there were perhaps 4/5 authors, one of which may have been a woman), he, she, they, wrote out of a particular cultural bias and were time-sensitive. All Biblical material can be examined in this light. Paul certainly had his particular bias and point of view, inspired or not.

Does this change the point of inspiration? I do not believe so. Inspiration still happens but does so contextually. I believe that certain truths are discerned from this inspiration, but we, in turn, must discern these truths from our own experience and relationship with God, as did the early writers of scripture.

Consequently, different perspectives and different points of view produce different facts about a given story. It does not mean that the facts are wrong in and of themselves. It only means that they reflect a given understanding of the writer relating the story from his faith community. For instance, the Creation story in Genesis has two renditions. Chapter one gives a seven-day account ending with the creation of man and woman. Chapter two, on the other hand, begins with the creation of man, then produced a garden where he placed man and then gave the man a helpmate, a woman. Factually, which one is true? They cannot both be if we look at them in terms of "inerrancy." Likewise, the birth narratives in Matthew and Luke tell the same story but with different facts. Mark and John omit a birth narrative. The same is true with the Passion (death/resurrection of Jesus) narrative. We hear the same stories, but the order of events, people, and places disagree. If we were to take the position, because the facts of these stories are confused, and thus, in error, then the whole Bible would be relegated to a false narrative. To assume that would be to miss the point of scripture.

Another issue with the Biblical narrative is with the copy and translation of the Bible. The Bible we have today has undergone a transformation since the original Aramaic, of which we have no original manuscript. The first English translation was done by John Wycliffe in 1385, which is almost 1300 years after the early ancient manuscripts. Prior to the English translation, it had been published in Latin, German, French, and a series of other idiomatic languages. In essence, what we have today is a copy of a copy of a copy of a copy of a copy of a copy of a translation, of a translation, of a translation, of a translation, of a translation, ad infinitum.

Most likely, the early manuscripts of the Mosaic law and Prophets were written in a dialect of Hebrew, though some scholars would argue for a more Aramaic dialect. When the Jews were transported into Captivity, though they may have been able to take some scrolls with them, someone made a translation into Aramaic, the main tongue of the Assyrians, their captors. The Aramaic translation was considered a word-for-word translation of Hebrew. In 285 AD, a Greek version of the Old Testament was translated from the Hebrew called the Septuagint.* This gave the Alexandrian world (Egypt, Rome, and Greece) exposure to the Jewish faith and was considered a refined and accurate translation.

In the later part of the first century AD, in the city of Edessa, in Mesopotamia, an ancient copy of the whole Bible was found, excepting the second and third epistle of John, 2 Peter, Jude, and Revelation. It was translated from the Hebrew into a Syriac dialect, namely, Aramaic. This translation was a prominent text in the Syrian/Aramaic communities.

In the latter part of the 4th century AD, Damascus, Bishop of Rome, appealed to St. Jerome, one of the greatest scholars of his day, to produce a Latin translation of the Bible, particularly the New Testament. Jerome meticulously went about his work, consulting the many translations available to him and produced his translation. For over a thousand years, it was heralded as the premier version of the scriptures in Western Europe. This was called the Latin Vulgate version, and it was Jerome who gave names to the various books bearing their names.

It was not until a thousand years later that John Wycliffe (England 1385 AD) produced the first English version of the Bible. It was quickly perceived as heresy. One hundred and forty years later, Tyndale published his English version of the Bible and was burned at stake as a heretic. Eighty-six years after that, in 1611, King James authorized his version of the Bible, which was basically 90% of the Tyndale translation. A lot of history, discussion, accused heresy, dissention, and rivalry happened in the years between all the different versions, and I left out several other important translations. New translations keep coming down the "let's make the Bible better" path, even to the present day. I'm sure you all have your favorite version of the Bible. I have several. For general reading, I like the New International Version (NIV) and Eugene Peterson's 'The Message' version. For a critical Greek translation, I like the New Revised Standard version, which is supposed to be a more accurate translation of the Greek and is also included in the Oxford Annotated Bible. The Oxford is my primary study Bible because of all the annotations that explain many of the verses with idiomatic explanations of Greek phrases.

This brings me to a primary issue of translation regarding idiomatic phrases, particularly in the original Aramaic, that cannot accurately be translated into Greek. The same is true from Greek to English. For instance, from Greek to English, in the *Gospel of Matthew 19:25,*

NIV, "It is easier for a *camel* to go through the eye of a needle..." I always thought the relationship between a needle and a camel was suspect. The Aramaic says it this way: it is easier for a *rope* to go through the eye of a needle. The Aramaic word *"gamla"* has three meanings based on its use, camel, large rope, and beam. In translation, camel and beam do not fit the essence of the Aramaic phrase. Of the three, which one would best go with the needle? There is an old narrative that says that there was a small gate in the wall of Jerusalem that required camel caravans to unload their camels to get through the gate. It was called the Eye of the Needle. There is no historical evidence that that was ever true.

Why is this important? Why not just believe the Bible is true and accept it on faith? Good question. My reason would be that the Bible is a living document, just as creation is a dynamic (living) event. God's creation didn't end in seven days. It is a dynamic event that continues even today. God is always at work. Likewise, the Bible, like all scripture, is a living document that breathes spiritual truth. This does not mean that spiritual truth continues to evolve. On the contrary, *it is our understanding of spiritual truth that changes with our journey in this life.* There have been many times that I have read scripture without any emotional attachment, and one day I reread it and, OMG, that's what that means! There is an old Eastern saying, "when the student is ready, the teacher will appear." That has been the story of my life, and I am so grateful for the many teachers that have graced my presence.

Why is all of this important to me? I have a passion for understanding the nature of things. Who wrote the Bible? Regarding the NT, in its original language, what was the intent of the writer, what is it he wanted his faith community to know about Jesus, and how do we know the words attributed to Jesus are, in fact, true? We may never know the actual answer to those questions until we cross over to the other side and can ask those questions. However, it may be that, on the other side, the whole conversation is irrelevant.

So, when all is said and done, what does all this mean? I can only speak for me. The core of any scripture is its spiritual truth, regardless of which faith community it comes from. In Christianity, I have found a lot of cross-over from the various other faith traditions, which to me, means that there is a core of spiritual truth that permeates the Universe that we all share. Intuitively, I know it does not make a lot of difference regarding the facts of scripture and whether the stories are literally true. What matters is my personal experience with the scripture and how it translates to my spiritual growth. In essence, it is how I experience Spirit Energy (God) and live out the truths as I understand them.

We must keep in mind that scripture is a faith document, founded not so much on facts, but on the perceived experience of the writer. Jesus scholar,

Marcus Borg, when asked, is the Bible true? He would always respond, *"Yes, the Bible is true, but all the facts aren't."* What difference does it make what the order of creation is, how it was done, or how long it took? The only necessary fact is that the event happened and that God did it! End of story. What we need to ask is what the event means to us? How does it affect our life experience? Nothing beyond that really matters. The same is true with the birth narrative and passion story. What difference does it make how it happened, and who was there? The important ingredient is that it did happen; how and when is inconsequential. Faith, I believe, is an experience of the event itself, not the facts. If we worship the facts, then we lose the experience, and in losing the experience, we build faith on the sand and not the rock of experience. I see most scripture as metaphorical.

I will pose this question, "what if the whole Biblical story is meant to be understood metaphorically rather than literally?"

I find it interesting that there is no historical text of figures in the Bible, outside of the Bible and Koran, that mention Abraham, Isaac, Jacob, Moses, Joseph, and the prophets. As important of a ruler/governor as Joseph was said to be in Egypt, you would think that somewhere in Egyptian hieroglyphs and writings, there would be a mention of such a hero to Egypt. You would also think the same regarding Moses. It is true that archeology and history can verify some of the kings, cities, states, and geographic places mentioned in the Bible. However, it also needs to be said that just because there is no proof outside of the Biblical material, it does not, in and of itself, make the Biblical story fiction. It does, however, cause me to wonder.

Scripture is a guide that shines through many windows. There is as much truth in the Torah, the Bhagavat Gita, the Koran, the Buddhist writings as there are in the Christian Bible. I have always appreciated the verse in *II Timothy, 3:16, NIV: "All Scripture is God-breathed and is useful for teaching, rebuking, correcting and training in righteousness (right-thinking)."* Notice that it says "ALL" scripture... When Timothy was written in the late first century, there was no designated scripture other than the Pentateuch, Prophets, and some of Paul's letters, maybe a gospel or two. There was no "Bible" yet so designated. The Bible was birthed at the Council of Nicaea in 325 (AD) under Constantine.

Therefore, I believe that scripture, from whatever source, is inspired but not the inerrant and literal truth or Word of God. We need to see scripture for what it is; as Spong says about the Bible, *"The Bible is a human book mixing the profound wisdom of sages through the centuries with the limitations of human perceptions of reality at a particular time in human history."*

Given this point of view, the question becomes, does this change the meaning of the message? I would say no.

Septuagint means seventy, which indicated the number of Alexandrian Jewish Scholars that translated it from the Hebrew. Each of the seventy was put in a separate room, did a complete translation of the OT, and when the translations were compared, they were so identical that the work was considered inspired.

THE VIRGIN BIRTH: AS THE MIRACULOUS AND LITERAL MEANS BY WHICH THE DIVINE NATURE OF CHRIST HAS BEEN GUARANTEED.

> "I do not think [the birth stories of Matthew and Luke] are historically factual, but I think they are profoundly true in another and more important sense…I do not see these stories as historical reports, but rather metaphorical narratives using ancient religious imagery to express central truths about Jesus' significance." - Marcus Borg

The story of Mary as the virgin mother of Jesus is problematic at best. I don't question the legitimacy of Mary as Jesus' mother; however, I don't believe it was a virgin birth, except perhaps in a metaphorical sense. Faith prescriptions can produce any kind of results, and most likely, that's what has occurred here. The virgin motif appears only in Matthew's and Luke's Gospel, and they are divergent in their telling. Mark, the first gospel, makes no mention, nor does John, the last Gospel. It is interesting that Paul, in all his letters and writings (that preceded the gospels), makes no mention of supposedly such an important edict of faith.

In Matthew 1:23, NIV, we read that a "virgin shall be with child…". The Greek word for 'virgin' is "Parthenos," which literally means "a young maiden."

Where did the 'virgin birth motif' come from? It has pagan influence, to be sure, and most likely was an edited 'proof text' scribed in Matthew's and Luke's Gospel in the later part of the first century AD. By this time in the development of the early church, it became necessary to justify Jesus as Messiah and genetic son of God. What greater way to do that than to prescribe a supernatural birth? Such a messiah, son of God, could not possibly have a natural birthright. Some pagan religions had already set the stage that such a phenomenon had possibilities. Christianity, through the ages, has not been afraid to borrow ideas from other sources.

We don't know what actually happened. The biological possibility of a virgin birth goes against every natural law we know in these times. We do know that the notion of the virgin birth was legitimized in 325CE at the Council of Nicaea with the formulation of the Nicene Creed.

Having said all that, it behooves me to mention another dimension of the Virgin Birth. There is written history, recorded in Hindu writings in India of a St. Issa (Hindu translation of Yeshua, Jesus...see Essay 14) that went about the countryside teaching and healing. Accordingly, this St. Issa was said to have had an immaculate birth, consistent with other Divine gurus throughout Hindu history.

I think it is clear that Jesus, Virgin Birth or not, possessed a spiritual quality born out by his Divinity. Is Jesus' Divinity unique? Actually, no more than yours or mine. We are reminded that Genesis tells us that we are created in the "image" of God. Whatever that image might be, all humanity shares its DNA. Jesus would be first to tell us that his divinity is no greater than ours. The difference is Jesus understood his divine nature and nurtured it. He was, in essence, as Dr. Allen McKiel likes to say, "Jesus is the very self of God made know." He became awakened to the work of the Holy Spirit. His whole mission was to encourage that awakening in us that we, too, might become sons and daughters of the Divine.

The central issue, it seems to me, virgin birth or not, does it change the message of Jesus? I would maintain not. I do not know that God would need to send a super, divine-human to do his bidding. Regular, created humans that are chosen, had done his work in the past, and I believe continue to do so with the manifestation of Jesus. We are reminded, "many are called, but few are chosen." God often sends messengers in the context of his creation of humanity, and Jesus was certainly one of them. Does the Christian faith pivot on the virgin birth motif? I do not believe that it does. For me, it is inconsequential.

JESUS, AS THE ONLY BEGOTTEN SON OF GOD

"For God so loved the world that God gave her only Son, so that everyone who believes in that one may not perish—spoil or rot like fruit here and now—but may have eternal life here and now. Indeed, God did not send the Son into the world to condemn the world, but that the world might be saved—healed, liberated, made whole here..." - Rev. Gusti Linnea Newquist

To answer this question, I refer you to the movie, "Oh God!", which starred George Burns and John Denver. When John Denver's character, Jerry, is put to the test by the theological council to prove that he actually talked to God, Jerry is put in a hotel room with a series of questions written in ancient Aramaic and Greek. When God, in the form of George Burns, finally comes to the hotel room, they begin going through the questions. One of the questions was, "Was Jesus the son of God?" God answers, "Yes, Jesus was my son. Buddha was my son. Mohammed was my son. Krishna was my son. You are my son, as was the innkeeper and the man who charged you an outrageous $11.00 for that steak." (Movie: Oh God!, 1977, Warner Bros.)

I rest my case.

What? What about John 3:16, NIV? "For God so loved the world that he gave his [only begotten] son...."

The 'only begotten son' motif is a theological issue that has been debated since the early days of Christian origins. It was finally codified in 325 A.D. at the Council of Nicaea with the Nicene Creed. It was Constantine at the Council of Nicaea, along with the council of Bishops, that insisted that the Nicene Creed would contain the translation as "only Son of God, eternally begotten of the Father" to insure the messiahship and literal sonship of Jesus. It was in this Creed that "the only *begotten" idea was formulated and made church doctrine. Here is that portion of the Nicene Creed: "We believe in one Lord, Jesus Christ,

the only Son of God,
eternally begotten of the Father,
God from God, Light from Light,
true God from true God,
begotten, not made,
of one being with the Father;
through him all things were made."

25

What is interesting, the phrase 'eternally begotten' is not a Biblical concept and is not found in the Bible. On the other hand, we are left with John 3:16, as one notion that "God gave 'his only begotten' Son...", to verify the idea that Jesus was God's physical offspring, in the same notion that Isaac was Abraham's begotten son.

What is unclear in this discussion is whether or not we are talking about the physical, human Jesus, or Jesus the Logos, the Word that was in the beginning. If we are talking about the Logos, then I would understand the 'Christ' as being the only begotten Son because he was in the beginning, as Genesis says. In the beginning was the "Christ, the very Self of God, the Christ, the very Self of God was with God and the Christ, the very Self of God was God. (John 1:1 metaphorically paraphrased.) This Christ Consciousness is the same essence as Krishna to Hinduism, Buddha to Buddhism, Mohammed to Islam, etc.

If we are talking about the physical, human Jesus, born between 6 BC-3 AD, then there can be no 'only begotten' because Jesus' birth had a beginning, not unlike any other human being. I would conclude that Jesus did not become Christ until his baptism by John. The three gospels, Matthew, Mark, and Luke, say as if in one voice, it was there (at baptism) that the heavens opened up and a voice said, "this is my son, the beloved...." There is nothing about 'the only begotten,' which would lead me to conclude that the sonship was a spiritual relationship.

The disagreement, whether or not Jesus is the 'only begotten,' rests on the meaning of the Greek word "monogenes." More traditional scholars, who support the King James version, lean toward the 'only begotten' translation. Other scholars imply that 'monogenes' indicates a 'uniqueness.' Dr. Rocco Ericco says, *"to clarify…the original Aramaic did not use the word "begotten." "…There is no "begotten" (Semitic root "yalad") in the Aramaic translation of 'monogenes' anywhere! (Dr. Errico Ricco, The Aramaic Gospel of John, 2006, p. 57)*

Tom Pittman "… suggests that "begotten" is not a significant part of the meaning of the Greek word (if at all). In every case, "unique" is the key element of the meaning, and most modern translations -- except the ones trying to hang onto the sonorous feel of the KJV -- correctly translate 'monogenes' as "only" or "unique." (Tom Pittman, Itty Bitty Computer Essays, June 11, 2016)

In the light of the Aramaic and Greek translations, I would believe that Jesus was not the "only begotten Son" but was "unique" in the context of birth and creation. Likewise, the sonship (and daughtership) of all God's people are unique and divine in that same way.

I believe this is also borne out by John in 14:12, NIV: *"Very truly I tell you, whoever believes in me will do the works I have been doing, and they will do even greater things than these…"* The inference here is that all of God's people that know and have experienced Christ Consciousness will do greater things than Jesus.

I believe that Jesus did not consider himself better than any other person. Jesus was chosen to express the "Christ Consciousness" to humanity and instill that All are God's unique children. Dr. Allen McKiel says it this way, *"Jesus is the very Self of God, made known, expressing Himself."* McKiel continues, *"the All-Possessing God is beyond knowing except as He makes Himself known, which the Greeks and later the Christians referred to as the Logos. God is both the Most Known and the Most Hidden. The Logos is how He makes Self known. The Divine nature of the Manifestations of God are human beings that perfectly reflect the Self of God in the Revelation of ongoing guidance for the social and spiritual evolution of humanity."* (Dr. Allen McKiel, Zoom Conversation, March 2021)

The first chapter of John, verse 12, says this, (literal Greek) *"But such as received him, to them gave he the prerogative to be children of God; [even] to them that believe on his name;"* Paul understood this relationship in his various letters, i.e., Romans 8:12-25, NIV; 9:6-8, NIV; Galatians 3:24-29, NIV; Ephesians 1:5, NIV; Philippians 2:8, NIV, I John 3:1-3, NIV; and Revelations 21:7, NIV. We ALL share the Oneness of Spirit of being 'unique children' of the Father, God!

In discussing the sonship of Jesus, we also need to address the misunderstanding of the idea that God and Jesus are one and the same. To speak of one is to speak of the other. The Evangelical community often interchanges God and Jesus in their prayers, litanies, and general conversation. This notion is further solidified in John, 10:30, NIV, *"I and the Father are One."* In my mind, God and Jesus are two distinct entities. Jesus often talked of God separate from himself. "Only the Father knows..." (Matthew 24:36, NIV), "There is none good but God alone..." (Mark 10:18, NIV). To me, the idea of oneness expressed in this verse is the fact that ALL God's people (creatures) are ONE. We all share the same DNA. What God birthed in Jesus was the "Christ Consciousness" that is expressed in each and every aspect of God's creation. We are divine, in the same manner that Jesus was Divine. However, we need to say that Jesus is the very Self of God made known with a capital D. Divinity is the image of the Creator that moves and lives in our being. So, I too can say that the Father and I are One.

*Something is begotten when it's been generated by procreation — in other words, it's been fathered. A somewhat old-fashioned adjective, begotten, is the past participle of the verb beget, which means to father or produce as offspring.

ATONEMENT: THROUGH THE DEATH OF JESUS ON THE CROSS, HIS SPILT BLOOD IS DEEMED A RANSOM FOR MANY.

"There never was a time when we were created perfect and fell into sin and needed to be rescued. We are evolving people; we are not fallen people. We are not a little lower than the angels. We're a little higher than the apes. It's a very different perspective."

- John Shelby Spong

Atonement maintains that through the death of Jesus on the cross, his spilt blood is deemed a ransom for many; provides cleansing of sin and heralds salvation to the believer.

I believe one of the most problematic issues of Christian theology is the doctrine of atonement, that the blood of Jesus cleanses the sins of many. To those that proclaim his death, their sins have been justified through the outpouring of Christ's blood in the cross. "Saved by the Blood," as the old hymn says, is a common cry of those who buy into the traditional language and theology. Most commonly, John 3:16, NIV is quoted, *"For God so loved the world that he gave his only begotten son that whosoever believes on him should not perish but have everlasting life."* Mark 10:25, NIV says that Jesus came as a "ransom for many."

One could ask, how does the blood do that? I suppose if we believe in a mystical, magical, theistic God, then anything is possible. Seriously, how does one man's blood cleanse the sins of many? Quite frankly, I have a hard time with the notion that Jesus died for my sins. Why would he do that? Yeah, I know, because the Bible says so. If there is anything that Jesus taught, it was accountability to God, *"Whatsoever YOU do..." "Do unto others as YOU...".* There is no evidence that God needed a sacrificial lamb to dispense his grace.

The Aramaic translation will give us a clearer understanding of this notion. In the King James Version, all references to this notion that Jesus died for our sins, or our "redemption" was saying that all humankind was redeemed from our sins by the spilt blood of Christ. The term "redemption" or "redeemed" means that someone made a payment or a "ransom" to someone else. It is often said that Jesus was a ransom for many (Mark 10:25, NIV). However, in the Aramaic, the word used for redemption is "mittol," which means "because of" or "on account of," which in English would mean that Jesus died "because of" our sins, not "for" our sins.

This makes a lot more sense to me. The sin of mankind crucified him. How often do our tongue and action metaphorically "crucify" the life of another? No greater Love..." "Love does not require the blood of an innocent to be shed for those who do evil. By simply turning to God— that is, by turning to good—one turns from evil and finds life and forgiveness. This is Jesus' teaching." *(Aramaic Light on the Gospel of John, Dr. Rocco Errico, 2002, p. 57)*

The other part of this belief for me is that the atonement motif is a carryover from Judaism; it connects the sacrificial system we see in the Old Testament to a God that could not do for God's self; what could be done via an intermediary sacrifice. Does that sound confusing? After all, the first converts to the new faith were Jews, and they were not initially called Christians but people of "The Way." If you recall in the book of Acts, Luke wrote that the early believers were called Christians at Antioch, and originally, it was a term of derision. We also have to remember that Paul's letters were written sometime in the '50s, and the gospels were written between 65 and 110AD, 25 to 75 years after the crucifixion. Ideas and faith experiences evolve over a period of time. Paul writes in I Corinthians 13 that when I was a child, I spoke and thought like a child, but I am no longer a child. I need adult beliefs that give me more understanding of myself and the world.

Over time it became necessary to justify the death of Jesus (Messiah in Hebrew, Christ in the Greek). Why would God kill the Messiah, as they understood Jesus to be? The justification came by the notion of "atonement," sacrifice if you will; people were not adequate enough in and of themselves to be accountable to God directly; hence, the elaborate system of atonement was set in place. A judgmental, theistic God needs an act of atonement so we (the created) can tell the difference between the forgiver and forgivee. This was part of the work of the Council of Nicaea in 325AD.

God, by definition, is love, peace, grace, goodness, possibility, and any other positive adjective you would care to suggest. God does not need an intermediary to dispense God's love or whatever God would care to give. It is accessible to all and every person that calls to claim it. You do not have to have a license, be a certain age, sex, height, weight, or have a college degree. You are by the very act of creation, worthy of God's love and all that God has to offer. Jesus spent three years in ministry telling us that.

Again, my take, John 3:16, is part of a mistranslation of the Aramaic text. I don't need Jesus to save me from my sin. I know that Grace is ever-present, and as Jeremiah

(31:34, NIV) said, "God remember their sin no more." To that end, I am grateful.

Are you ready for this? We are NOT SAVED by the actions of God or Jesus, but by OUR own actions and often thoughts. We are, in truth, the only means whereby salvation can occur. Granted, it emanates from God, but we must claim it through our own forgiveness, right-thinking, and right acting. God has no notion to forgive because God does not condemn. Even though Grace is free, we still feel that we have a need to ask forgiveness. God does not say in return, "Go, and be forgiven!" "He/She says, Go, and sin no more."

This point of view, of course, negates the idea of original sin. Just as one man's blood cannot save many, likewise, one man's sin does not condemn many. The Adam and Eve story is metaphorical and is about disconnection from the God source. We can thank St. Augustine of Hippo (4th century) for formulating the idea of original sin. Prior to the fourth century, it was not a fundamental notion of the early faith.

We are accountable for our sin and, likewise, accountable to resolve it by making the necessary correction in our life. This is where we ask God for wisdom and understanding to make that correction. The spiritual journey is one of staying connected, even though life's obstacles try and disconnect us.

May your connection to the spirit be worthy of your faith journey.

THE PHYSICAL RESURRECTION OF JESUS AS PORTRAYED BY THE EMPTY TOMB AND THE APPEARANCE STORIES AS TOLD BY THE GOSPELS, MATTHEW, LUKE, AND JOHN.

"I don't think the Resurrection has anything to do with physical resuscitation. I think it means the life of Jesus was raised back into the life of God, not into the life of this world, and that it was out of this that his presence" — not his body — "was manifested to certain witnesses." - John Shelby Spong

According to Paul, the essence of the Christian Faith rests on the resurrection. In I Corinthians 15: 13, 14, NIV, Paul writes these words: *"If there is no resurrection of the dead, then Christ has not been raised; and if Christ has not been raised, then our proclamation has been in vain, and your faith has been in vain."* What is not clear is whether Paul is referring to a physical or a spiritual resurrection. Later, in the same chapter, Paul discusses the various bodies *"it is sown a physical body but is raised a spiritual body."* The implication here is that if Jesus was resurrected, he was done so in a spiritual body. On the road to Damascus, Paul seemed to have experienced a spiritual Jesus.

There was no actual witness to the resurrection, only the fact that the tomb was empty. Depending on the particular gospel you cite, the women (the gospels do not agree on who and how many) came to the tomb and observed that the stone had been rolled away and the tomb was empty. Since women in this culture and period were chattel or second-class citizens, it is interesting that the gospel writers give women the first rite, as witnesses, to the empty tomb. If credibility is to be had, it would seem that men would have been more credible because when the women ran to tell the men, the men did not believe them but had to go see for themselves. On the other hand, there is a distinct (diabolical) intention by having women as the first witnesses.

Besides the empty tomb, the only other evidence lays

in the post-resurrection appearances. Matthew and John have Jesus appearing at the tomb; Mark, in the original ending* (verse 8), has no post-resurrection appearances. Matthew and John describe appearances in Galilee, yet Luke limits Jesus' appearance to Jerusalem. The writers also differ in how they describe the resurrected Jesus. Luke and John depict him in concrete physical terms. They describe Jesus as eating and inviting a doubtful disciple to touch his wounds. Paul's risen Christ, on the road to Damascus, was more of a spiritual Christ. The evidence is inconclusive at best.

"Abdu'l-Baha', eldest son of Bahá'u'lláh, the founder of the Baha'i faith, and successor to the Baha'i faith following his father's death, has said this about the resurrection of Jesus:

> *"The resurrection of the Manifestations of God is not of the body. All that pertains to Them—all Their states and conditions, all that They do, found, teach, interpret, illustrate, and instruct—is of a mystical and spiritual character and does not belong to the realm of materiality." (Some Answered Questions, 'Abdu'l-Baha,' 1908, Kegan Paul, Trench, Trubner & co.)*

What we do know is that something happened in the hearts and minds of the disciples that changed the course of human history for the next 2000 years. My personal faith does not hang on the necessity of a physical resurrection. Whether physical or spiritual, Jesus' teachings are not affected one way or another. Teachings born of love and Spirit live forever in the hearts and minds of the students.

If we presume our oneness in God, that we are all part of the eternal creative process, bodies come and go, but the eternal spirit that lives in each one of us does not die with the body. If something does not die, is it fair to call it resurrection if it still lives? We know that Jesus' body was executed, but his spirit (soul) was not. Crucifixion cannot kill the eternal spirit; death cannot kill the eternal spirit; because to kill the eternal spirit would be to kill God, and that IS IMPOSSIBLE!

If it was, indeed, a spiritual resurrection, then the term itself, 'resurrection'** is really a misnomer because the word resurrection means to come back to life. If the spirit is truly eternal and lives both prior to and after a physical birth and death, then that spirit/soul has not been resurrected because it has always been and always will continue to be. Taken from a spiritual perspective, there was no resurrection, just a simple manifestation of eternality. Jesus lives because death could not contain him; his spirit is eternal, the same as ours are; therefore, Jesus did not die. However, his physical body did return to dust.

There is another aspect of resurrection that is

metaphorically true; every night, we close our body down only to reawake, resurrecting ourselves to a new day with new opportunities and experiences to serve the greater good.

I have no doubt that the disciples saw the post crucified Jesus. The issue of physical or spiritual is of no consequence to me because I live by the spirit, and I know by the spirit that Jesus yet lives!

SO, WHAT DO WE DO WITH THE EASTER STORY?

> "I cannot say my yes to legends that have been clearly and fancifully created. If I could not move my search beyond angelic messengers, empty tombs, and ghostlike apparitions, I could not say YES to Easter." - John Shelby Spong

I am not sure we have to do anything with the Easter Story. It is what it is. However, having said that, I would change the emphasis. Since I do not believe that Jesus' death was a ransom paid for our sins, I have little use for the week leading up to Easter Sunday. Jesus' death was a tragic display of injustice, typical of the historical times. It was about power and spiritual truth. The Jews were afraid of his popularity and heresy of the faith. The Romans were afraid of insurrection, so the two powers of

Jerusalem were probably united for the first time about the necessary demise of this rag-a-muffin prophet. In real time, it was nothing more than getting rid of an inconvenience.

To me, the cross is a negative symbol of the Easter story. It is a symbol of death. I used to wear crosses, had a major collection of them. I no longer need that symbol to let people know that I am a part of the Christian community. If my actions and words do not speak the truth in loving kindness, then no metal or wooden symbol will change that.

The Easter event, the resurrection, continues to be a reflection of God's grace through the notion that Jesus yet lives! As the Apostle Paul said, death could not contain him. The physical body expires, but the spirit soars, giving us the promise that we, too, live eternally. That, in my mind, is the story of Easter.

* Textual critics have identified two distinct alternative endings: the "Longer Ending" (vv. 9-20) and the unversed "Shorter Ending" or "lost ending," [1] which appear together in six Greek manuscripts and in dozens of Ethiopic copies. Modern versions of the New Testament generally include the Longer Ending, but place it in brackets or otherwise format it to show that it is not considered part of the original text. (Wikipedia)

**Resurrection means a 'raising up' or 'rising up' from the Greek word ANASTASIS. In the verb form, it means 'to cause to stand or rise up; to raise from sleep or from the dead.' (Britannica.com)

THE SECOND COMING...?

"There is one thing to be suggested by the season of
Advent in the liturgical year that we are celebrating.
The theme of Advent is the two comings of Christ.
During Advent, we remember the first coming of
Jesus, even as we prepare for his second coming. And
the second coming occurs each year at Christmas,
with the birth of Christ within us, the coming
of Christ into our lives. Christ comes again and
again and again and in many ways. In a symbolic
and spiritual sense, the second coming of Christ is
about the coming of the Christ who is already here."
- Marcus Borg

So, what about the second coming of Christ? There
are 100 verses in the New Testament that speak
directly and indirectly to the second coming of Christ.
I have no intention of listing them all here but will share
a few of the more known verses.

Hebrews 9:28, NIV So Christ, having been offered once to bear the sins of many, will appear a second time, not to deal with sin but to save those who are eagerly waiting for him.

John 14:3, NIV And if I go and prepare a place for you, I will come again and will take you to myself, that where I am you may be also.

Revelation 22:20, NIV He who testifies to these things says, "Surely I am coming soon." Amen. Come, Lord Jesus!

1 John 3:2-3, NIV Beloved, we are God's children now, and what we will be has not yet appeared; but we know that when he appears, we shall be like him, because we shall see him as he is. And everyone who thus hopes in him purifies himself as he is pure.

1 Thessalonians 2:19-20, NIV For what is our hope or joy or crown of boasting before our Lord Jesus at his coming? Is it not you? For you are our glory and joy.

The second coming of Christ is a fundamental principle of Christian theology and a component of the faith. Without the second coming, the death and resurrection of Christ mean nothing. At the crucifixion, the Disciples could not believe that their teacher, whom they believed to be the Son of God, had been put to death on a Roman cross. Even though Jesus had given them a warning, which they obviously did not understand, they were completely distraught over the event. What do we do now? was the question at hand.

The fundamental believers will say that Jesus predicted his death, resurrection, and coming again. There are scripture verses attributed to Jesus that they claim clearly give that intention. The question I have is, considering the fact that Paul's letters and the Gospels were written some 30 to 60 years after the crucifixion, and even after 70AD when Rome decimated the temple and Jerusalem, how do we know what the real words of Jesus were? We know that there was an oral tradition that circulated around the various faith communities about what happened. The individual Gospels are a testament to similar stories but different facts. By the time the gospels were written, it is most likely that none of the Disciples were alive to witness their writing. Granted, the four gospels are named after Matthew, Mark, Luke, and John. Interestingly, all are anonymous, as far as we know. Although, whoever Luke was, seems to also author the Book of Acts. Most likely, these authors are not the people we think they might be. It is possible that John, the beloved Disciple, wrote the book bearing his name, but it's more likely he did not because the Gnostic flavor does not seem consistent with what we know of John. What we do know, regardless of who they really were, they each represented a particular community of the faithful, similar stories, different facts.

In spite of the second coming references, I am not compelled to believe that Jesus, the Christ, will return again in the flesh as he did in the first century. However, he might well come as a different messenger for our time in history. Some scholars believe that Jesus, the Christ, was the reincarnation of Elisha, and his cousin, John (the Baptist), was the reincarnation of Elijah. Elijah, whose story is found in the book of Kings, was God's prophet during the reign of Ahab in the 9th century BC. When Elijah was taken up by the swirling wheel of lights (alien spaceship maybe?), Elisha, Elijah's disciple, took up the prophetic mantle left by Elijah. It is interesting how the life of Elisha resembles the life of Jesus, eight centuries apart. God has certainly provided other messenger in the like of Buddha, Krishna, Mohammed, Moses, Zoroaster, Baha'u'llah, and others.

Back to the second coming, most likely, if there is a return of Christ, it will be in the form of a new and different messenger. And no, Donald Trump is not that messenger! Baha'is believe that their founder, (mid-1800s) Baha'u'llah, is the messenger for this current generation.

My contention is that the second coming of Jesus, the Christ, is meant to be metaphorical, not literal. There is the historical Jesus, born between 6 BC and 3 AD. The birth of the Christ Consciousness, the spiritual reality of the Kingdom of God born within all creation, was revealed at Jesus' baptism. Therefore, the second coming of the Christ Consciousness is when, in the words of the Evangelicals, "we accept Jesus as our personal Savior." When we realize that God, being Spirit, resides within the core of our being, or soul, as it were. It is that awakening and desire to live fully in that awakening that the Buddhists continue to strive for, and likewise, every Christian. The teachings of Jesus provide the divine path for awakening to occur. Have you witnessed the second coming yet?

ESSAY #8

HEAVEN AND HELL: AS PLACES OF ETERNAL REWARD/PUNISHMENT

"Hell is known as the eternal separation from God's
presence, while Heaven is eternal unity with God."
- Paul Tillich

Near-death experiences (NDE) have become more common in the 21st century. Mainly because people are telling their stories without fear of being chastised or called crazy. Many studies have been done on NDEs. Doctors have witnessed NDEs for many years. Now doctors are having their own NDE's and writing books to share their experience giving credibility to the whole NDE event.

It is interesting that, in most cases, the stories are similar. They often involve an out-of-body experience. People have experienced major heart attacks and find themselves on the ceiling watching the doctors work on their bodies. In most cases, they are swept away by a light or journey toward a bright light. Once they get there, they feel warmth and love like they have never felt before. Some meet family members, while others have met Jesus. Many are called back into the body, even though they want to stay in the light. Once they return, they say that they no longer fear death because they have experienced what they call heaven and the Divine. Likewise, there are a few stories that have negative consequences and others that experience nothing at all.

All this simply confirms there is life on the 'Other Side.' No one has mentioned "streets of gold" or "fires of hell," which leads me to say, heaven and hell, as understood by Christianity, are not what we presume them to be. Actually, the notion of streets of gold and fires of hell were popularized by the writings of John Milton in Paradise Lost and Goethe's Faust. There is no geography where heaven and hell are located. They are not a place up there or down there. Point of fact, someone pointing to "heaven" in Australia is pointing in the opposite direction of someone in the Artic.

Most likely, we get our notion of hell as a 'hot' place from the reference in Matthew 5:22. Here, the teaching of Jesus takes an interesting turn. One who is angry with his brother/sister will be in danger of the judgment. If you insult a brother/sister, you will go before the council, but should you call your brother/sister a 'fool,' you will be liable to the fires of hell. The point here, I believe, is that you shouldn't even think negative thoughts toward another.

The literal translation of the word hell in Greek is 'Gehenna,' which was a valley outside of Jerusalem associated with a religious pagan rite.

It eventually became a garbage dump where trash was burned, including bodies, that over time was a hot, smoldering, smelly place. To wish someone to go to Gehenna was not a pleasant thing! The consequence of one's anger is an obsessive burning desire to wreak revenge on the perpetrator. Jesus was saying that as long as you carry that anger, it will burn your insides out as if you were standing in the fires of Gehenna.

Now I realize that this argument does not resolve the notion of what hell is or is not. At some point, each individual must interpret for themselves what hell is or is not. I like the definition that Jean Paul Sartre gives in his play, "No Exit," "Hell is other people." How true for many of us. At any rate, the notion of hell, as far as I am concerned, is only a state of mind that we often find ourselves in when we lose sight of our divine nature and purpose. It's a state of mind we inflict on ourselves and each other.

It is almost humanly impossible to think of our sins without forgiveness.

Our greatest condemnation comes not from God but from ourselves. God has no need to forgive us because he/she does not condemn us. We condemn ourselves because we don't believe that we are worthy of God's love. So, the act of forgiveness that is essential here is that we must forgive ourselves. And that, my friend, is often the most difficult thing we ever have to do. Because our love is not perfect, it often needs forgiveness from ourselves and from others that we have harmed in some way.

Given this point of view, what is there to say about the Day of Judgment?

If we accept the fact that God does not condemn, then that sort of eliminates any kind of Day of Judgment. The Biblical literature is full of holocaustic images of the Day of the Lord, or the Day of Judgment when supposedly God reigns down God's terrible sword on unsuspecting humanity. This whole doomsday theology is an attempt of an ancient culture trying to understand the mystical images they saw and/or experienced in an attempt to understand God. It is certainly not a part of my understanding of God or my reading of the Biblical material.

I don't believe that God goes about capriciously snuffing out the life of impenitent sinners. God honors God's creation. I believe when God had finished with the six days of creation, he looked around and said, "Hey, this is good, this is very good." And, so it is. What humankind has done to it, however, is another matter.

Heaven, likewise, is not a place up above the clouds

somewhere. It is a dimension of spirituality that resides in the ethers of God's presence. It is not a place of reward, nor a place reserved only for 'saints.'

I believe that heaven is found on this earth plane. It is a dimension that lives next door to us. It is a state of consciousness that often overwhelms us, gives us goosebumps when we see a newborn baby, a beautiful sunset, a smile or a hug, a timely touch that is reassuring, or words of comfort; and enjoy frivolity and laughter, a big piece of apple pie with vanilla ice cream, playing music, singing loudly, watching a hummingbird, or watching children play. Prayer and meditation can take us deep within, knowing we touched the Spirit, found our soulmate, or our first cup of coffee in the morning, ad infinitum.

I strongly believe in life afterlife. There is no such thing as death per se because we are spiritual beings having a body experience on this earth plane. The body is mortal; the soul is not. The soul never dies. It is without end. Elizabeth Barret Browning said in one of her poems, *"Life is perfected by death."* I've always liked that quote and have used it in many memorial services. In a sense, death ties a bow around the body on this lifetime, claiming the body is done for now. The physical maladies that you have accumulated over this lifetime are released; there is no judgment, in a sense, your journey has been perfected. However, once on the other side, you will still continue your soul work.

Once the body dies, what happens to the soul? It is immortal and goes to an eternal realm in the presence of God. Once on the "other side," the soul continues its spiritual work, or *karma (soul journey) if you prefer. You may choose to have another life experience.

For instance, if in this life experience you encounter a person that is the antithesis of everything you are and creates stress and paranoia, you do everything you can to avoid this person. He/she always seems to show up at the most inopportune times, making your life miserable. If you never confront this person or try to resolve your issues, this person, in a different body, will most likely show up in your next reincarnation and will continue to do so until you learn the soul message of how to make it right. Do you have anyone like that in your life now?

The universe (God) is always giving us the opportunity to do soul work. Chances are, also, that you will have family and friends follow you into your next lifetime. Another aspect of this journey is that some believe that we choose our parents, basically because of what we feel we need to learn, to progress our soul journey.

Everyone that has ever lived, regardless of how they have lived their life experience, will go to the 'Other Side.' There is no hell to go to; there is no heaven with pearly gates, just the beauty in God's presence. As the NDEs proclaim, we will experience a light and love that goes beyond our imagination. We will be given the opportunity to review and evaluate our last life experience to see where we need improvement on our soul journey. There may well be some soul work to be done, for a longer period of time, on the other side, before we can reincarnate, should that be our choice.

So, if there is no heaven or no reward, what is the point? The point, obviously, is to honor and serve our divinity. Live life fully and exaggerated, love unconditional and with reckless abandon. Take care of the earth and be a servant to others. Or, in the words of Micah 6:8, What does the Lord require of you, but to serve justice, love mercy and walk humbly with your God. Therein is heaven.

* Karma (car-ma) is a word meaning the result of a person's actions as well as the actions themselves. It is a term about the cycle of cause and effect. According to the theory of Karma, what happens to a person, happens because they caused it with their actions.

WHAT'S THE DEAL
WITH SATAN?

"Christians have…identified their opponents, whether Jews, pagans, or heretics, with forces of evil, and so with Satan…Nor have things improved since. The blood-soaked history of persecution, torture, murder, and destruction perpetrated in the name of religion is difficult to grasp, let alone summarize, from the slaughter of Christians to the Crusades, to the Inquisition, to the Reformation, to the European witch craze, to colonialization, to today's bitter conflict in the Middle East." - Elaine Pagels

This is an essay that I would prefer not to write. I find the subject matter tiresome and boring. Nonetheless, it is an important topic because it offers Evangelicals someone to blame for their miscues and misdeeds.

Back in the early seventies, comedian Flip Wilson

performed as a character called Geraldine on his TV show. One of Geraldine's favorite expressions was, "The Devil made me do it."

I will say it forthwith: I do not believe in Satan. I do not believe that Satan exists as an opposing force of God that makes us do things we don't want to do.

As the myth goes, in classical Christian 'Satanology', Satan (also called Morning Star, Lucifer, the Devil, Beelzebub, and the adversary) was an archangel and was one of God's most blessed creations. He/she/it had the power of being God's most trusted angel. "Some accounts of this myth, say that God cast the archangel out of heaven because he would not honor Adam, the first man created by God. When the jealous archangel refused to acknowledge "a lowly thing made of dirt," God punished his/her/its pride by throwing him down into hell. There, as Satan, the fallen archangel ruled over a kingdom of devils, former angels who had followed him/her/it in his fall." *(Myths Encyclopedia.com. internet)* This fall from heaven myth is also found in Babylonian and Canaanite mythology.

The first question that comes to mind for me is, why would God create something like Hell? According to the myth, hell had been created because God didn't seem to hesitate to throw Satan 'down there'. And, if you believe in a *theistic God, then it would be necessary to have a place to punish disobedient believers or non-believers

55

as it might well be. A jealous God would need an outlet like Hell to appease his ego need.

As I indicated in an earlier essay regarding Hell (Essay #8), there is no Hell outside of the imaginations of John Bunyan and Goethe's Faustus and the dogmatic faith-building of the Middle-Ages church.

Is Satan real? Assuming that Hell is a myth, then there is no need for a Satan. Metaphorically there is, but as a real entity, no. *In early appearances of the word "Satan," when literally translated from Hebrew, simply meant "adversary. "None of the [Hebrew] passages that use the word refer to an inherently evil spirit." (Dr. Henry Kelly, Professor of English Research, UCLA, 2006)*

It is unfortunate that Christianity was developed as a dualistic religion/philosophy. Basically, that means that because you have one thing, you must have the other. If there is an up, there must be a down. If something can be opened, it must also be closed. If there is light, there must also be darkness, and so on. Dualism is also part of the Gnostic philosophy.

However, duality is the nature of our culture. From God's point of view, there is only oneness. In the spiritual realm, there is only the idea of one. God is love. God only creates love. God is completeness in and of him or herself.

God gave us "free will," the ability to make choices about how we live our life's journey. We can choose to live it singularly in spirit or dualistically, with one foot in light and the other in the darkness. The greater good is not always seen or understood in a way that makes "right-thinking" and "right-action" a worthy choice. The spiritual path requires discipline, and the easier choice is to follow ego, that which feels good and that which looks good. As Jesus replies in Matthew 7:13-14, NIV, *"Enter through the narrow gate. For wide is the gate, and broad is the road that leads to destruction, and many enter through it. But small is the gate and narrow the road that leads to life, and only a few find it.)* Hence, our conscience allows us to choose the wide path, duality over the singularity of oneness with God. We, therefore, consciously choose which side of the duality we will live in or, as the wisdom story of the two wolves, which wolf we will feed.

We can say that the dark side of this duality is the "adversary," the other voice in our head that encourages us to take the shortcut, to not follow the rules, to say no one's going to know, I'm better than you, or I can do what I want. Historical Evangelical Christianity has called that voice the voice of the devil or Satan, who is always out to get us, just waiting to pounce and carry us off to his hellish abode.

This metaphorical Satan is the voice that says we need to be fearful of strange ideas, even strangers…, people who look different from us. It is a voice that seeks to separate us from family and friends. It is a voice that keeps us longing for the "good ole days" and fearful of the future. This voice we hear is not a voice external to ourselves but a voice that we recognize because it is our voice. It is a voice sometimes controlled by the delusion of our thoughts and mindless demeanor. If you hear that kind of a voice saying, "Let's riot the Capitol and kill members of congress and the VP," it is not God's; it's your voice. If a voice you hear asks you to kill somebody in the name of God, trust me, it is not the voice of God. God does not seek to destroy his creation but continues to create in Love. God is not a God of violence, regardless of what you might believe about the Old Testament. There is an old spiritual song called "Shut De Dor, Keep Out de Debil." We might well remember that song when that voice in our head begins to play tunes that we know in the core of our being are delusional.

* Bishop John Shelby Spong calls this "theism" and argues that this is a *"…human definition, not a divine revelation"*. Spong continues, *"the theistic God in these various traditions (Islam, Judaism, and Christianity) was always other, always external to the self who was defining the God-figure, always supernatural, and, at least in the West, usually personal in the sense that individuals could know and communicate with this deity. The theistic God was also presumed to be the explanation for that which was beyond rational understanding, a being capable of miraculous power who therefore needed to be supplicated, praised, obeyed and pleased."*

Essay #10

LET'S TALK ABOUT EVIL...

"There are two ways to be fooled. One is to believe what isn't true; the other is to refuse to believe what is true." - Soren Kierkegaard

Volumes have been written about the nature and presence of evil. The full text of this book could discuss evil and never answer all the questions to anyone's satisfaction. I have no intention of taking that on except through this essay that expresses my core belief about evil. What I don't cover could well be fodder for another book, though I doubt it.

I find that I resonate with the teachings of 'Abdu'l-Baha,' an early 19th-century leader of the Baha'i faith on evil:

"In creation, there is no evil; all is good. Certain qualities and natures innate in some men and apparently blameworthy are not so in reality. For example, from the beginning

of his life you can see in a nursing child the signs of desire, of anger, and of temper. Then, it may be said, good and evil are innate in the reality of man, and this is contrary to the pure goodness of nature and creation. The answer to this is that desire, which is to ask for something more, is a praiseworthy quality provided that it is used suitably. So, if a man has the desire to acquire science and knowledge, or to become compassionate, generous and just, it is most praiseworthy. If he exercises his anger and wrath against the bloodthirsty tyrants who are like ferocious beasts, it is very praiseworthy; but if he does not use these qualities in a right way, they are blameworthy. ... It is the same with all the natural qualities of man, which constitute the capital of life; if they be used and displayed in an unlawful way, they become blameworthy. Therefore, it is clear that creation is purely good."

('Abdu'l-Baha', Some Answered Questions, 1930, Baha'i Publishing Trust)

"Evil is non-existent; it is the absence of good; sickness is the loss of health; poverty the lack of riches. When wealth disappears, you are

poor; you look within the treasure box but find nothing there. Without knowledge there is ignorance; therefore, ignorance is simply the lack of knowledge. Death is the absence of life. Therefore, on the one hand we have existence; on the other, nonexistence, negation or absence of existence."

('Abdu'l-Baha', Foundations of World Unity, p. 76-79)

We know absence of light is darkness, but no one would assert darkness was not a fact. It exists even though it is only the absence of something else. So evil exists too, and we cannot close our eyes to it, even though it is a negative existence. We must seek to supplant it by good, and if we see an evil person is not influenceable by us, then we should shun his company for it is unhealthy.

Shoghi Effendi, Lights of Guidance, p. 512

A response to evil that I like is from an old Cherokee wisdom saying:

"One evening, an elderly Cherokee brave told his grandson about a battle that goes on inside people.

He said, "my son, the battle is between two 'wolves' inside us all.

One is evil. It is anger, envy, jealousy, sorrow, regret, greed, arrogance, self-pity, guilt, resentment, inferiority, lies, false pride, superiority, and ego.

The other is good. it is joy, peace, love, hope, serenity, humility, kindness, benevolence, empathy, generosity, truth, compassion and faith."

the grandson thought about it for a minute and then asked his grandfather: "which wolf wins?"

the old Cherokee simply replied, "the one that you feed."

(Nanitcoke Indian Tribe-Delaware)

I believe, like the Baha'is, that God's creation is good. Evil is not something that comes from the act of creation itself but from the physical realm of human existence. Evil is the consequence of bad choices.

"Does this mean that evil does not exist? No— it means evil has no existence of its own.

Consider the shadow of an object. That shadow only comes into being in the area where the object obscures light. The shadow has no existence of its own, for without the object there would be no shadow. Therefore, we can say that the shadow is non-existent, when compared to the object; however, we cannot deny the existence of the shadow."

(Oliveira, Morco. How do You Define Evil? baha'iteachings.org. December 12, 2014)

Evil is non-existent, except in the presence of the human mind. Goodness is our dominant trait, but the path of goodness is tempted by many detours along our journey. In one sense, it is that God allows evil; otherwise, our choice would have no merit. To say that God allows it does not mean that God creates it.

So it is that God blessed us with a sense of 'free will,' the ability to make choices about our life. That's right, choices. Religious culture has interpreted those choices as good and evil. The allegory told in Genesis of Adam, Eve, and the Serpent (can also be expressed as Freud's Id, Ego, and Superego*) is basically the same as the two wolves. God did not create evil but allows it to play out as a choice that we humans make. Hence, we have in every religious faith tradition, teachings to help us stay on the divine path.

What happens if we don't stay on the path?

I don't believe a loving God condemns anyone to something like hell. If we presume that God is the very nature of goodness, the very nature of love in all senses of the term, then it would seem to me that God, as divine goodness, and divine love, does not condemn. Love does not condemn. Paul, in his letter to the Corinthians, reminds us (chapter 13) of this very fact. So, if we take this logic to the next level, we will have to say that God has no need to forgive. Yes, that's what I said; God has no need to forgive! Why doesn't God need to forgive? Because God does not condemn. If there is no condemnation, there is nothing to forgive. However, even though God has no need to forgive, his/her grace is "given for" us. God does not condemn us, damn us or judge us harshly. God loves us unconditionally. Jeremiah (31:34) tells us that God does not remember our sins. Why is that? Because God does not condemn us for our sins. God's concern is that humans make good choices, and even though we don't always do so, God knows that our soul conscience will be the mirror of our actions. Life is a process of choices, and we don't always choose the lesser good, but the door to God's love is always open for spiritual growth.

* According to Freud's psychoanalytic theory, the id is the primitive and instinctual part of the mind that contains sexual and aggressive drives and hidden memories, the super-ego operates as a moral conscience, and the ego is the realistic part that mediates between the desires of the id and the super-ego. (internet)

THE GOSPEL OF THE KINGDOM OF GOD

"The task of religion is not to turn us into proper believers; it is to deepen the personal within us, to embrace the power of life, to expand our consciousness in order that we might see things that eyes do not normally see." - John Shelby Spong

I have always been drawn to the scripture of Mark 1:15, which claims that Jesus came preaching the gospel of the Kingdom of God. I've always wondered what the gospel of the Kingdom of God was. It does not seem to be spelled out in a way that is obviously understandable. I think we can assume that it was not "Christ crucified." So, what was it, what is its meaning?

We can possibly assume that it was about a gospel (Good News) of Love, Compassion, and Mercy. Those are quite general notions that have a broad translation.

It wasn't until I read Parmahansa Yogananda's, The

Kingdom of God chapter in his book, "The Yoga of Jesus Christ," that new insight on the 'kingdom within' came to light. If we look at Luke 17:21, we get a clear clue about the kingdom of God within. The literal Greek says it this way, "*Nor will they say, behold, here or there; behold for the kingdom of God within you is.*" There is some scholarship disagreement with the word 'entos' which most commonly translates *'within,'* but other scholars translate *it 'in the midst of,* or among' which implies that the kingdom of God is not necessarily within, but in the midst of, which would insinuate that Jesus, as the messenger of God, was the one in the midst of.

However, right or wrong, I would argue that Jesus came preaching that the Spirit of God is not out there somewhere but lies within the 'inner-being' of humanity. It is not something we can find external to ourselves, but is, in essence, the core of our being, what we call the soul. It is innate in every human being, hence, created in the 'image' of God.

If that is, indeed, the case, what then might we say about 'the Kingdom of God within'? How do we understand it as a guiding principle in our life? The Christians say that you need to accept Jesus Christ as your personal Savior (a salvation experience), and once you do, the Spirit of God is awakened, and you are transformed into a new being with a spiritual direction. The Buddhists see it as an 'awakening,' becoming aware of your being as a unique soul experience and committing yourself to a mindful and conscious journey on the noble eightfold path*. More precisely, the Buddha says it this way, *"The Way is not in the sky; the Way is in the heart."*

*The Noble Eightfold Path of Buddhism:

1: Right understanding (Samma ditthi)
2: Right Thought (Samma sankappa)
3: Right Speech (Samma vaca)
4: Right Action (Samma kammanta)
5: Right Livelihood (Samma ajiva)
6: Right Effort (Samma vayama)
7: Right Mindfulness (Samma sati)
8: Right concentration (Samma samadhi)
(Wikipedia)

Jesus reaffirms the Luke 17:21 notion in the Gospel of Thomas, Translated by Steven Davis (verse 3): *"If you think the Kingdom of God is above you, then birds will find it first. If you think it is in the ocean, then fish will discover it before you do. Look…the Kingdom of God is within you and all around you."*

The Bhagavad Gita via Krishna (from Hinduism) says it this way: *"With one's heart focused on yoga (union) and recognizing all things as equal, then you will see the Self within—and within all beings…See me in all things, do not become separated from me. I dwell in all things.*

Lao Tzu in the Tao (Dow) Te Ching says it like this:

"One can know the world without ever leaving home. The Way can be recognized without a window."

Even in the Old Testament, the Jewish Prophet Ezekiel claims, *[26] I will give you a new heart and put a new spirit in you; I will remove from you your heart of stone and give you a heart of flesh. [27] And I will put my Spirit in you and move you to follow my decrees and be careful to keep my laws. (Ezekiel 40:26-27, NIV)*

I believe that the Kingdom of God within is a universal spiritual principle that lies at the core of ALL religious traditions. It makes the case that there is one God, one principle of Love, Compassion, and Mercy that precedes the fundamental truths of all the great religions-One God, many paths. In my youth, I could never understand why a God of Love would only provide one path to find him/her. It just didn't make sense to me. I would think that God would make it 'easy' for everyone to find him/her. Each path has its own merits and means of providing the spiritual path to nirvana. Metaphorically, it is like some people choose to drive a Ford, others a Chevy, still others a Cadillac. It does not make any difference what kind of car you choose to drive as long as you are on the divine path. I believe that no single religious tradition encompasses all spiritual truth but that all traditions have a part of that truth, and all traditions together, comprise the whole truth.

So, having said all that, what does the Kingdom of God within mean?

The core of our being is found in the stardust of the universe created over thirteen billion years ago with the Big Bang if you please, or through divine creation if you must, though, they are one and the same. It imposes the likeness or 'image' of God that we find in the creation story in Genesis. What is that likeness? It can only be one thing, LOVE! It is out of love that we are created and out of love that our divine purpose is given.

Believe it or not, God has one life plan for everyone, all humans…and that is to love with reckless abandon. It doesn't make any difference what our life path is, the career we have chosen, our skillset, whatever it is, in whatever we do, love with reckless abandon! (*7 Dear friends, let us love one another, for love comes from God. Everyone who loves has been born of God and knows God. 8 Whoever does not love does not know God, because God is love. 12 No one has ever seen God; but if we love one another, God lives in us and his love is made complete in us.) (I John 4:7,8,12, NIV)*

Buddha offers 4 elements of Divine Love:

Loving kindness. Offering joy and happiness.

Compassion. The intention and capacity to relieve and transform suffering and lighten sorrow.

Joy. Well-being, gratitude, peace, and contentment in the mind in the here and now.

Equanimity. Nonattachment,
nondiscrimination, even-mindedness, or
letting go.

Hinduism: What sort of religion can it be without compassion? You need to show compassion to all living beings. Compassion is the root of all religious faiths. (Basavanna)

Tao Te Ching: I have three treasures. Guard and keep them:

> The first is deep love. The second is frugality; the third is not to dare to take the lead in the empire.

Islam: A man once asked the Prophet what was the best thing in Islam, and the latter replied, it is to feed the hungry and to give the greeting of peace both to those one knows and to those one does not know." (The Hadith of Bukhari)

This aspect of Divine Love is also found in the Golden Rule:

CHRISTIANITY: Whatever you wish that men should do to you, do also to them. (Matthew 7:12, NIV)

ISLAM: Not one of you is a believer until he loves for his brother what he loves for himself. (Forty Hadith)

JAINISM: A man should wonder about treating all creatures as he himself would be Treated. (Surrakritanga)

CONFUCIANISM: Try your best to treat others as you would wish to be treated yourself, and you will find that this is the shortest way to benevolence. (Mencius)

HINDUISM: One should not behave toward others in a way that is disagreeable to one's self. This is the essence of morality. All other activities are due to selfish desire. (Mahabharata)

BUDDHISM: Comparing oneself to others in such terms as "Just as I am so they, just as they are so am I," he should neither kill nor cause others to kill. (Sutta Nipata)

Of course, we are talking about unconditional love, a love defined by the Greek word "agape": *but if we love one another, God lives in us and his love is made complete in us. (I John 4:12, NIV)*

And so, it is that the Gospel of the Kingdom of God is the 'kingdom within' and/or the Christ Consciousness that is ever-present, exampled by love.

It is a spiritual teaching and journey we all must take on our own; would that I could give it to you, but I can only concern myself with my own spiritual journey. Putting into practice Micah 6:8, NIV, *"What does the Lord require from you, but to serve justice, love mercy (compassion) and walk humbly with your God," is also a good beginning.*

JESUS AS THE ONLY WAY TO GOD, "I AM THE WAY, THE TRUTH AND THE LIFE, NO ONE COMES TO THE FATHER EXCEPT THROUGH ME." JOHN 14:6

"So, Jesus is "the way." What does this metaphor, applied to a person, mean? We need to ask, "What is Jesus' 'way' in John's gospel?" Or, "What is 'the way' which Jesus is?"

- Marcus Borg

"The church meets to imagine what our lives can be like if the gospel were true."

- Walter Brueggemann

I have always found this verse to be a little disconcerting. I cannot understand why Jesus would say something so exclusive. It is this verse that the Evangelical community uses to prove that Jesus Christ is the only way to God, which implies that Christianity is the only one true faith. It has also been a verse that has been used through the ages to justify intolerance to those who were not Christian.

Dr. Marcus Borg, of the Jesus Seminar, maintains that Jesus did not say the words found in 14:6, and, most likely, none of the words found in the Gospel of John. Even more likely, this gospel was not written by John. Though it appears with his name, John the son of Zebedee, and Jesus' most trusted disciple. John was likely beheaded by Agrippa I, around 44AD. The writing of the Gospel of John took place in the late part of the first century or early 2nd century. This gospel has *gnostic overtones, which would leave one to believe that the writer came from the gnostic community.

However, just to say that Jesus did not really say the verse in question doesn't really excuse it. If we look at the Aramaic, translated by Dr. Rocco Ericco, we get a similar translation of the Greek, literally translated into English, reads: *"*Yahweh (I AM) is the truth, the way, and the life. No one of you here comes to the Father but through me.*"** However, there is a little different emphasis. The "I AM" (ego eimi, in Greek) does not reflect a personal "I" but more of a cosmic I, like the great "I AM THAT I

AM." This would lead one to say that it is not Jesus who is the way, etc., but the very self of God, hence, Yahweh. So, it would translate as such: *"Yahweh (not Jesus) is the way (or road) the truth, and the life."* The second part of the verse, *"No one of you here comes to the Father but through me."* This particular translator believes that Jesus was talking specifically to the disciples (no one of you here), comes to the Father but through me.

Now we can argue over the specific meaning of this part of the verse. Based on what I understand about Jesus and his teachings, I don't believe that he would intentionally say something so exclusive as the father could only be experienced through Him. How does one do that? Does that mean we tear a hole through the chest of Jesus and fight our way through to find God? Facetious, I know.

I have to look at this part of the verse metaphorically. That would mean that Jesus was the manifestation of God's love and the only way to the Father is through that Love. I don't believe, for a nanosecond, that Jesus would be so egotistical to say that only through him is there a way to God. That would mean that all of the faith traditions that had come before him, Hinduism, Buddhism, Taoism, Zoroastrianism, and others were all for not. They each had their own path to God that expressed a deep spirituality. I don't believe that Jesus would have thrown them under the Bus!

So, believe what you will, I see this verse through the

eyes of a metaphor, Love. Interestingly, we keep coming back to Love. Must be a reason!

* Gnosticism's Christian form grew to prominence in the 2nd century A.D. Ultimately denounced as heretical by the early church, Gnosticism proposed a revealed knowledge of God ("gnosis" meaning "knowledge" in Greek), held as a secret tradition of the apostles. In *The Gnostic Gospels*, author Elaine Pagels suggests that Christianity could have developed quite differently if Gnostic texts had become part of the Christian canon. Without a doubt: Gnosticism celebrates God as both Mother and Father, shows a very human Jesus's relationship to Mary Magdalene, suggests the Resurrection is better understood symbolically and speaks to self-knowledge as the route to union with God. Pagels argues that Christian orthodoxy grew out of the political considerations of the day, serving to legitimize and consolidate early church leadership. Her contrast of that developing orthodoxy with Gnostic teachings presents an intriguing trajectory on a world faith as it "might have become." *The Gnostic Gospels* provide engaging reading for those seeking a broader perspective on the early development of Christianity. - *"The Gnostic Gospels" written by Elaine Pagels, reviewed by F. Hall.*

**This Aramaic translation comes from Marco Caceres Di Iorio, in a November 2005 article in IDSENT, online.

SOME THOUGHTS ABOUT PRAYER

"The function of prayer is not to influence God, but rather to change the nature of the one who prays."

- Soren Kierkegaard

"Some people think prayer stops bullets, rockets or land mines. It doesn't. That's magic. That's not God. Sometimes, you're just in the wrong place at the wrong time."

- John Shelby Spong

I was listening to a televangelist talk about prayer. Many, if not all, of the televangelists are Evangelicals and have their TV home on TBN, the Trinity Broadcast Company. This pastor was a "good ole southern boy" not only by his claim but his southern drawl. He was talking about how prayer is greatly misused and misunderstood. I began to take notice. He said one of the notions used about prayer is the fact that God is considered stupid because the prayer has to include every minute detail of the request. His example went something like this: We come to you today, O Holy One, because one of our families is in real dire needs. I'm sure you know the Olsen family that lives down by the RR crossing in the old brown house with the shingled roof receding and a stack of tires out front along with an old chassis of a car. I think the car is an old chevy that was once red but doesn't hold me to that. Mr. Olsen works down at the local feed store and is a good and trusted employee, and he loves you, Lord. The Olsen's have five kids, three girls and two boys. I don't know their names off the top of my head, but if you hold on, I will get them for you. I'm sure somebody here in the congregation would know those names. And so, the prayer goes…Who does this pastor think he is praying to, a mindless Sugar Daddy?

None of the information in the prayer is necessary outside of the fact that the Olsens need help. I'm sure in time, the prayer would get to the request part. If God knows anything, he knows the Olsen's and their situation. We are told God knows our needs before we ask.

The internet says this about the real meaning of prayer:

> "Prayer is a way of being: being in the
> moment, being present, being open. It is

a way of learning to be ourselves. For the theist, it is learning to be in the presence of God, a presence that infuses every moment and every space – but one to which we devote our attention on order to encounter the Divine."

For the Christian, what is the biblical meaning of prayer? (via the internet)

"Prayer in the Hebrew Bible is an evolving means of interacting with God, most frequently through a spontaneous, individual, unorganized form of petitioning and/or thanking. ... In these instances, such as with Isaac, Moses, Samuel, and Job, the act of praying is a method of changing a situation for the better."

The Christian Church recognizes four basic elements of Christian prayer: (1) Prayer of Adoration/Blessing, (2) Prayer of Contrition/Repentance, (3) Prayer of Thanksgiving/Gratitude, and (4) Prayer of Supplication/Petition/Intercession. Some prayers will include all four elements; others may be only one or two. There are no rules regarding how many elements you

must have in your prayer, but it should be
said that if your prayer is to be 'legitimate,'
you would be wise to follow and use any of
the four elements of prayer.

Matthew 6:5-13, NIV provides what we have, as to
an actual formula for prayer, believed to be taught by
Jesus himself, identified as the Lord's Prayer:

Our Father, who art in heaven,
hallowed be thy name;
thy kingdom come, thy will be done
on earth as it is in heaven.

(Adoration/Blessing)

Give us today, our daily bread
And forgive us our trespasses, as we forgive those who
trespass against us.

(Contrition)

And lead us not into temptation;
but deliver us from evil.
(Petition//Supplication)
For thine is the kingdom,
the power and the glory,
for ever and ever.
Amen.

(Thanksgiving/Gratitude)

Far be it from me to argue against this formula and its author. I have no problem with this formula for prayer. It is a good outline for many Christian folks to follow. Part of my problem is not with the prayer itself but how it is often used that concerns me. It seems that most prayers are long on "petition," "Lord, give me..., Lord make me...Lord, heal me..." and short on contrition and thanksgiving.

Bible scholar Karen Strong says, *"We talk about God as though he was like a somebody. We ask him to bless our nation, or save our Queen, or give us a fine day for the picnic. And we actually expect him to be on our side in an election or war, even though our opponents are also God's children."* John Shelby Spong says it this way, *"Most prayers assume that God is an external being, possessing supernatural powers. Prayer is thus often seen as the activity of last resort. "There are no atheists in foxholes," we are told. We assume that this deity has the power to manipulate the forces of nature to bring about a desired result. Our prayers seem to assume that God might not "do good" or "be merciful" unless we ask God to do so. Our prayers also seem to assume that the mind of God can be changed, and with it the course of history. Do we really want to think that our prayers have that power?"*

What is really at issue here is our understanding of God and how we interpret the notion of prayer. The late

German Theologian, Paul Tillich, said that, in essence, God does not exist, but rather, is the "ground of all existence." God is not a being, but is, being itself. It is easy to make believe that God is a being because it allows us to talk to God like a real person. However, how do you communicate with being itself? Therein is the delusion of Christian prayer.

I want to tell you what I have learned about prayer. It is not about petitioning God for things. I know there are scriptures, *"...whatsoever you ask, I will give it to you" (John 14:14, NIV)* that offer misleading notions about what God can and will do. Paul reminds us in I Thessalonians 5:17, NIV to "pray without ceasing." This does concern me. In essence, we must keep praying for what we want in hopes that God will change his/ her mind about our request, just in case he/she didn't hear us the first 50 times! Why wouldn't one request be adequate? After all, it is God, and he/she surely doesn't forget. It could be we think God grades on a scale and whoever gets the most requests in during a certain time period wins the trophy, er, a, the request.

I do not believe God to be capricious and randomly answers prayers.

I believe that the most honest prayer we can express is through the nature of our being. A new translation of the New Testament, The Passion Translation (2017), translates I Thessalonians 5:17 as "Make your life a prayer." Our life becomes the prayer by the way in which we understand and live out our spiritual being. For our life to be a prayer means that we must make our spiritual journey dedicated to the task of, no less than Micah 6:8, "What does the Lord require of you, but to serve justice, love mercy and walk humbly with your God." This, I believe, is what Paul meant by "pray without ceasing."

I have become very particular about how I want people to pray for me. I never want people to pray for my healing of cancer, congestive heart failure, and other maladies that gather around me. If you have a need to pray for me, I ask that you pray for only two things: Wisdom and Understanding. Pray that I receive the wisdom and understanding to deal with whatever situation that might befall me. I believe that we have to allow the universe, 'God' to work in his/her way as only he/she can do. If we confine God with specific requests, we limit our ability to see the bigger picture. Let God decide how he/she will interact in our life; all we need to do is get wisdom and understanding. God will do what God's going to do. If we pray too specifically, we may lose out on God's truth for us. After all, we are told that God knows our needs even before we ask (Matthew 6:8, NIV).

When I pray for others, I request the light of Spirit to surround the person or persons and ask Divine Spirit to provide wisdom and understanding during this time on their spiritual journey. Let it be so. At night, before I fall off to sleep, I pray, "I release, loose, let go and let

God." This allows me to clear my mind and start each day with Psalm 118, "This is the day the Lord has made, I will rejoice and be glad in it."

I believe that one of the most important prayers we can offer is prayers of gratitude. There are so many things to be grateful for, regardless of our situation. Paul reminds us about that fact when he says, *"Give thanks in all things."*

Thirteenth-century mystic, Meister Eckhart, said it best, *"If you only have one prayer to give, let it be a prayer of thanksgiving!"*

I am always saying thank you to Spirit, the Universe-God, when little things happen on my behalf. Somethings I get to go through an intersection on a green light before it changes red, and that's a thank you! Sometimes I get a parking space close by, that is a thank you! Sometimes I'll forget what I am doing, and after a few moments or so, the memory kicks in, and that's a thank you! There are times when I say thank you for the pain because it is a reminder that I am still alive and have the opportunity to do great things...well, maybe just do things. I say thank you at night for the blessings of the day when I crawl into bed.

The most important thing about prayer is that it is not really about God or Spirit, but it is about us. What we understand to be true and how we see ourselves at that moment. Our prayers do not change the mind of God, but they can change us, especially when they come from the core of our being. Prayer is very much a part of our soul work. The best prayer is one that comes from the heart. Words need to be our words and our thoughts. If the notion of prayer troubles you, go back to the prayer of Jesus and let that be your guide.

In closing this essay, I share with you one of my favorite prayers from St. Francis:

Lord, make me an instrument of your peace.
Where there is hatred, let me sow love;
Where there is error, truth;
Where there is injury, pardon;
Where there is doubt, faith;
Where there is despair, hope;
Where there is darkness, light;
And where there is sadness, joy.

O Divine Master, grant that I may not so much seek
To be consoled as to console;
To be understood as to understand;
To be loved as to love.
For it is in giving that we receive;
It is in pardoning that we are pardoned;
It is in self-forgetting that we find.
And it is in dying to ourselves that we are born to eternal life. Amen.

The petition that St. Francis is asking here is not about physical or social gain but about spiritual truths for our spiritual journey. Let it be so.

Meditation is often aligned with prayer, though I believe, the Christian tradition has a problem with meditation. I have often heard that prayer is talking to God, meditation is listening to God. Therein, I believe, is the problem. Many Christians have a problem listening, period!

Meditation requires a sense of mindfulness. To sit quietly in a comfortable position; clearing the mind of extraneous thought; monitoring your breath, in and out; being present in the moment; allowing yourself to experience the silence of God.

The Zen Buddhist tradition of Thich Nhat Hahn encourages walking meditations, particularly in nature. Since we are a part of the universe, a walking meditation through nature allows us to become One with the source of eternal being. We hear the songs of birds, the rustle of the leaves and grass, chirping of frogs and insects, all expressing their joy in creation, and welcoming us into their domain.

I haven't been able to actively do a walking meditation for some time now but that does not deter my ability to meditate wherever I am. Sometimes it's only for a few minutes but there is a sense of oneness with all creation that empowers the silence and the feeling.

Many people use mantras, (words, phrases, poems,

scripture, etc.) to help center oneself into meditation. From a Christian perspective, I would suggest the Lord's Prayer, any of the Psalms or other scriptures that speak to you. If you want to get serious about meditation, I suggest a book titled, Practicing Mindfulness, Finding Calm and Focus in everyday life, by Jerry Braza. Jerry is a master teacher in the Zen Buddhist tradition. This book does not teach you to become a Buddhist but teaches you mindful meditation which is universal to all faith traditions.

Meditation is an art form like playing and writing music or writing poetry.

It is a mindful connection you make with the universe/creation and expresses the oneness of all things, living and inanimate. Like salvation or enlightenment, it can't be explained but only experienced. There is a point in the spiritual journey where prayer and meditation merge together, they become one and the same thing. That's because, at the core of their essence, they express divine love. It is so dynamic that it can't be held in thought but only expressed in action. That action being serving the greater good and being in service to others.

If you haven't already, I hope you find a meaningful journey in meditation.

ESSAY #14

BELIEVE IT OR NOT, THE LOST YEARS OF JESUS

> "[P]eople need to use their intelligence to evaluate what they find to be true and untrue in the Bible. This is how we need to live life generally. Everything we hear and see we need to evaluate—whether the inspiring writings of the Bible or the inspiring writings of Shakespeare, Dostoevsky, or George Eliot, of Ghandi, Desmond Tutu, or the Dalai Lama." - Bart D. Ehrman

Little is known factually about the lost years of Jesus, the period between 12 and 30 years old. There are no historical facts that provide a narrative about those lost years. However, there are many legends and myths about Jesus in India, Tibet, Japan, and Great Britain.

What we do know is from the Gospel of Luke, second chapter. Jesus is presented in the Temple at Jerusalem for purification (circumcision). Afterward, the family returned to Nazareth, and there, Luke tells us the *child grew and became strong; he was filled with wisdom, and grace was upon him."* (Luke 2:40, NIV) Following in verse 52, Luke NIV tells us that *"Jesus grew in wisdom and stature, and in favor with God and man."*

Biblical scholars, particularly those that study the historical Jesus, are adamant that Jesus went nowhere near the far east and even smirk at the idea. Instead, they say that Jesus spent his middle years helping attend his father's carpenter shop in Nazareth, "growing in wisdom and stature."

I have to confess that I am intrigued with the stories, myth or not, involved in these middle years of Jesus. The evidence seems every bit as compelling as stories in the Gospels and other pseudo writings of the late first, second, and third centuries. The fact that you have four gospels that share similar information gives credibility to the Biblical narrative on the life history of Jesus. However, there is nothing in the four gospels about the middle years. It was a Russian war correspondent, Nicolas Notovich, circa 1877, who visited Hemis Buddhist Monastery in Ladakh, India, where he was told of a scroll titled, "Life of St. Issa, Best of the Sons of Men."*

From Wikipedia…"According to the scrolls, Jesus abandoned Jerusalem at the age of 13 and set out towards Sind, "intending to improve and perfect himself in the divine understanding and to studying the laws of the great Buddha." He crossed Punjab and reached Puri

Jagannath, where he studied the Vedas under Brahmin priests. He spent six years in Puri and Rajgirh, near Nalanda, the ancient seat of Hindu learning. Then he went to the Himalayas, and spent time in Tibetan monasteries, studying Buddhism,[32] and through Persia, returned to Jerusalem at the age of 29." Notovich, after an accident with a broken leg, was returned to the monastery for recovery, and while there, had the scroll translated and copied. In 1894, he published the copy in French. Though it was greeted with some interesting reactions, it was later considered fraud and hoax, which made Notovich a laughing stock.

From Wikipedia, "In 1922 Swami Abhedananda, the founder of Vedanta Society of New York 1897 and the author of several books, went to the Himalayas on foot and reached Tibet, where he studied Buddhist philosophy and Tibetan Buddhism. He was one of the skeptics who tried to debunk Nicholas Notovitch and disprove the existence of the manuscript about Jesus in India. However, when he reached Hemis monastery, he found the manuscript, which was a Tibetan translation of the original scrolls written in Pali. The lama said that it was a copy and the original was in a monastery at Marbour near Lhasa. After Abhedananda's death in 1939, one of his disciples inquired about the documents at the Hemis monastery but was told they disappeared."

If you journey the path across India, supposedly

taken by St Issa, you will hear story after story of this great saint from town to town that you visit.

Guru Parmahansa Yogananda (1893-1952), who brought meditation and **Kriya Yoga to the west, also talks about Jesus' journey through India as St Issa in his writings, "Autobiography of a Yogi" and his two-volume work, "The Second Coming of Christ and the Resurrection of the Christ within You."

So, what do you think? Fact or fiction?

There are also Hindu (India) references to the birth of Jesus, particularly as it relates to the "wise men." Ancient Hindu scrolls indicate that the "wise men" were actually from India and not Persia. Historically, it is believed that the "wise men" were Zoroastrians from Persia. Point of fact, there were Zoroastrian believers in India at the time of Jesus. As the legend goes, the "wise men" from India brought gifts of gold, frankincense, and myrrh. These are traditional gifts that would be offered to newborns in the Indian culture. The legend believes that when Jesus went to India, he did so at the bidding of the wise men who helped him settle in their country. This will be a discussion for another essay; believe it or not.

The English form of the name "Jesus" is derived from the Latin Iēsus, which in turn comes from the Greek Ἰησοῦς (Iēsoû-Yay-soos). The Greek is a Hellenized form of the Hebrew name Yēšua (יֵשׁוּע), which is, in turn, a shortened form of Hebrew Yᵉhōšua (יְהוֹשֻׁעַ) or "Joshua" in English.[1]

Aramaic (Classical Syriac) and East Syriac, which are ancestral to West Syriac, render the pronunciation of the same letters as ܝܫܘܥ ishoʿ (išoʿ) /iʃoʕ/, Issa) (Wikipedia)

**Kriya Yoga is an ancient philosophy that helps to accelerate spiritual development.

WHAT DO WE DO WITH THE CHRISTMAS STORY?

"Christianity may be surprised to learn that there are different versions of the cherished Nativity story that we tell and retell. This is due to the varying interpretations that are present in the New Testament. There are two accounts of the first Christmas that offer differing details and context for which it occurred. Many people are unaware that Luke and Matthew offer completely separate genealogies regarding Jesus." - Marcus Borg

There were no witnesses to the birth event of Jesus. All we have are the oral traditions, some myth and folklore, and the accounts of the gospel of Matthew and Luke. By the time Matthew and Luke got around to writing their accounts (late '70s, early '80s CE), a great deal of oral tradition had been passed around. This would have been thirty-five plus years after the death of Jesus and about 70 plus years from his birth, assuming

3CE as that date. A generation of stories had most likely been created and passed around to justify the divine origin of one believed to be the Son of God.

Interestingly, Matthew and Luke tell different stories about the birth. Both, however, place the birth in Bethlehem. From Matthew's account, one would suppose that Mary and Joseph lived in Bethlehem prior to the birth. Luke, of course, has them traveling to Bethlehem from Nazareth due to a Roman census requiring families to register in the place of their descendants. Joseph, being a descendant of David, traveled to the city of David—Bethlehem. Since it is presumed that Jesus grew up in Nazareth, Luke's account at least makes the connection. Current scholarship, in some cases, argues that Jesus was most likely born in Nazareth. Interestingly, there is no record in Roman history that a census had occurred during the period of Jesus' birth.

It is not my point to ravel through the Matthew and Lukian accounts to determine which account is most accurate. We will probably never know. My intention is to look at the Christmas story in the light of 21st-century scholarship and knowledge and consider what it means for Christians in what Marcus Borg calls the "emerging paradigm" of Christianity for the 21st-century. (The Heart of Christianity, Marcus Borg, Harper-2003)

In a previous essay, I have already discussed the virgin birth motif. I don't wish to belabor this point except to say that I lean away from the "virgin birth" notion.

The story is a timeless story both in beauty and poetry. It is true in a sense. Did it happen the way the gospel accounts imply? Were there shepherds and wise men? The answer is yes and no. The spirit of the story is true, but the actual events are not. In essence, it doesn't matter whether it is literally true or not. Jesus was born. As God does with every birth, God instills with each soul the full capacity of God's Love. The uniqueness of Jesus is that he was able to understand that Love and was able to imitate that Love and express that Love in a way that made people do a "double-take" when they heard or met him. He expressed the very Self of God. In a real sense, people had a better understanding of God after experiencing Jesus. As Paul would say, we put on the "mind of Christ" in our daily walk. We experience in Jesus, the Christ, the very consciousness of God's deep abiding Love that pervades God's presence, which of course, means to always do the best we can, wherever we can, and to whomever we can.

Christmas then becomes the celebration of this Christ consciousness in our life that is not bound by limitations of fact or myth but touches kings and shepherds alike with the same Spirit. And once you have experienced this Christ, angels will indeed sing, "Peace on earth goodwill towards all people!"

ESSAY #16

RACISM AND BIGOTRY!

"We must learn to live together as brothers [and sisters] or perish together as fools."

- Dr. Martin Luther King, Jr

"I look at American Christianity and I'm almost in despair. I don't want to be identified with it. The Christian vote in America is an anti-abortion, anti-homosexual vote. I consider that to be anti-female and anti-gay, and I don't want to be identified with a God who is anti-anything."

- John Shelby Spong

In good conscience, I cannot ignore cultural racism and bigotry in the Christian tradition. It is a fact of life in this decade of the 2020s. First, I will admit that I am a racist. Not because I consciously work at it, which I don't, but because I have been raised in a culture of white privilege. I can drive down the street without fear of profiling or being shot. I can walk the neighborhood in a 'hoody' without being stopped by the police. I can walk through a large department store without being followed by security.

Second, I am ashamed of what the white community of privilege has done to 'people of color' and to the LGBTQ+ community in the name of God! Who the HELL do we think we are?

I'm going to tell you a story. During the act of creation, God and the angels were considering how to create the perfect human. God configured out of clay what he thought would work and put the clay in the oven. The timer went off, and they ran to the oven expectantly, only to find that the human clay was not quite done having a pale white color. So, they tried it again. They added some time to the timer in hopes of a little better outcome. When the timer went off, God came to check. He opened the oven door only to find that the human clay was a nice black. He was admiring his work when an angel looked and said, "Oh my, I think that's too dark; we must try it again." And so, they did. This time they watched with anticipation, having set the timer not quite so long. This time the clay came out a nice light brown/yellow color; it was a genuinely nice color, but they thought they could still do better. Once again into the oven, this time it came out a nice warm brown. The angels thought it was magnificent, but God felt he needed to try it again. And so, he did. This time it came out a nice brown-red. God thought, "That is close to perfect. The angels agreed. As they looked at all the work they had done, God said." It is good to have different colors of humans for they will energize creation and make the family incredibly unique."

Obviously, depending on who is telling the story will determine which color will come out perfect. The point here is that there is equal equity in all the colors of the human race. All are equal in God's sight. Do you remember the children's song we used to sing in Children's choir, "Red and yellow, black, and white, they are precious in his sight, Jesus loves all the children of the world."

I will say it again; I am so ashamed of what the white community has done in the name of God to those who do not share white skin. Consider the 400 years of slavery, which frankly, even today, is still prevalent in our society. Not that we buy and sell blacks, but we impoverish them to a life of subsistence. If that doesn't work, we put them in prison for crimes for which whites only get a slap on the wrist. During WW2, we put American Japanese in concentration camps. We treated the Native Americans as strangers in their own land, slaughtered them, put them on a reservation, to what end? Only because they were an inconvenience to white privilege and progress.

I wished I could snap my fingers and make all prejudice and bigotry go away. I've tried it, but to no avail. For some reason, God continues to ignore the snap of my fingers (LOL). The best I can do is make sure that I honor, treat, and respect ALL people under the umbrella of equality. But, even more importantly, I must strive to act and acknowledge that ALL people are treated with the same equity. I don't believe, for a nano-second, that God favors white privilege. It could be that those with white privilege are the Pharisees of our generation's time.

Let me try and say it this way; there is nothing under the sun of God's creation that deserves privilege. Privilege lives in the realm of duality, them and us. God's creation is a unity of one. It doesn't matter the color, the culture, the gender, sexual preference, the size, the individual attributes (eye color, hair color, if any at all, left or right handedness} ad infinitum. There is only the ONENESS of God. Our DNA expresses that oneness as unique children of God.

I know, the Bible says…gays are an abomination to God (Leviticus 20:13, NIV). Yes, I know the Bible says that, but we must remember when that part of the Bible was written, some 500 to 600 years before the birth of Christ. Culture and understanding were a lot different than they are now. It's true that there are some references of homosexuality in the letters of Paul. But hear this: In Deuteronomy, chapters 21 and following, there are some interesting Biblical laws. In chapter 21, from verses 18 through 21, if your rebellious child does not obey, you can take him down to the city center and have elders stone him. I don't think we do that anymore. 23:1, if a male's penis is cut off, he is no longer admitted to the general assembly. I'm not sure how such an act could happen, but nonetheless, it does make you an outcast. 23:24, You have permission to go into your neighbor's vineyard and eat your fill but cannot take anything away with you. Again, in today's world, we would be arrested for trespassing and theft. 21:11, you cannot wear clothing weaved out of wool and linen together. Exodus 21:7 says it's okay to sell your daughter as a slave. These are cultural mores that do not fit into the 2020s. Why should we ignore these but feel obligated to obey Leviticus 20:13? What about Jesus? To my knowledge, Jesus never said, when confronted by a blind person or someone with leprosy, before I heal you, what is your position on gays and lesbians? Or abortion? Or racism?

So, which of the Biblical laws are we going to honor? Most of the Biblical laws were made in response to religious and cultural mores and are time-sensitive. Does that mean that to be true Bible believers, we must assimilate that old culture into our own present culture? I don't think so.

Our religious evolution behooves us to make the teachings of antiquity relevant for the 21st century. The spiritual truth of all religion, like the golden rule, are all the same and unchanging. What changes is the cultural context. For instance, in Corinthians, Paul tells women to cover their heads. There are cultures today that still do that. The reason Paul told women to cover their heads was that every night, a thousand temple prostitutes of Aphrodite invaded the city. In order to not be treated as a prostitute, Paul told Christian women to cover their heads, so people will know that they are not one of the Temple prostitutes. That is context.

To cut to the chase here, I believe that a God of pure love does not condemn ANY of his creation. It doesn't matter the color or sexual preference; all is good with God.

MY LIFE WITH B.U.G.S.
(BURDEN, USEFULNESS,
GRATITUDE, SPIRITUALITY)

"I have found I had less and less to say, until finally,
I became silent, and began to listen. I discovered in
the silence, the voice of God." - Soren Kierkegaard

Growing up in the Willamette Valley, I spent
many years in 4-H all the way through college.
When you sign up, you must choose a project. Most
of the other kids in my club were farmers, so they had
animals as their project. My family members were not
farmers, so I didn't have animals to choose from. I did
try woodworking and learned a few skills. When I was
about 13, Oregon 4-H offered a new program in the
field of Entomology, the study of insects. Not sure why
that interested me, but it seemed like a worthy program
to invest in. I suppose, if truth be told, my girlfriend at
the time (now my wife) was really into 4-H. She was
nationally honored with her sewing. Anyway, I figured
if I wanted to hang around with her, I needed to find a

4-H project, and entomology seemed like a nice way to go. It created a pathway through 4-H for me.

This entomology project required catching bugs and displaying them in a formal and specific manner. You had to find insects from a variety of family/order (genus/species) as you could; the more variety, the better your opportunity to score high and win a ribbon. Once you caught your bug, you would put the bug in a jar of formaldehyde* to put to sleep–permanently! Once the formaldehyde did its job, you would stick an entomology pin through the thorax of the insect and also write a tag with the insect's name and Latin family order. For instance, butterflies belong to the order of Lepidoptera. So, on a small tag, as tiny as you could write legibly, would be the name of the butterfly along with its Latin order name. Butterflies were hard to catch, and the crème de crème, was the tiger swallowtail, a yellow and black beauty. Equally hard to catch were dragonflies. I did win several ribbons and many blue ribbons for my insect displays. The summer between my junior and senior year in high school, I had my own Entomology club. I had three members, which included my sister. That summer at the state fair, my sister got state champion in her division, the two others received blue ribbons, as did I. I believe that was the last year I did Entomology. My succeeding years were involved with 4-H leadership.

So, aside from a brief history of 4-H entomology, what does this have to do with anything?

Thank you for asking.

In essence, my life journey has been about BUGS. BUGS has become an acronym for my journey. Four values that have been important to me are BURDEN, USEFULNESS, GRATITUDE, and SPIRITUALITY.

BURDEN

I have never wanted to be a burden to anyone or anything, though given the nature of our technology today, I'm afraid I have been victimized by my computer and cell phone. Nonetheless, burdenhood is not something that seems to fit with my soul. More specifically, it is most likely a carryover from my Evangelical/fundamentalist upbringing. I remember hearing repeatedly, be a servant, deny yourself and put others ahead of you. In the words of Paul, I Corinthians 7:23, NIV, "You were bought with a price, do not become slaves of men." Sometimes, it's funny how a young mind works. I have been a worthy giver but a reluctant receiver. What can I do for you? How can I help you? What? What can you do for me? Not a thing, I'm good!

The full extent of this notion of burden comes to rest with the fact that many families I have dealt with in ministry, because of severe injury or major medical issues, brought great burden to the family. Family members wasted away in a nursing home, for sometimes years, with no quality of life. Even more sadly, children, perhaps because of guilt, think that they need to keep their family members at home. Caregiving is one of the hardest jobs in the world. Of course, it is an admirable quality to care for a failing parent. Having seen this situation repeatedly, I do not want to be a burden to my family when that time comes. The wear and tear on a family caregiver is often beyond expectation, and in many cases, the caregiver passes before the patient.

I do not want my wife or children to have to bear that burden. If I am bedridden and cannot take care of my most basic functions, then throw me in a nursing home and let the professionals deal with me. Better yet, if possible, I will consider physician's assisted suicide. I am not afraid of death but more afraid of a body without any quality of life wasting away for sometimes years!

To be sure, there is a difference between burden and servant, and I choose being a servant over being a burden. I would hate to think that my psychosis of burdenhood overwhelms my desire to be a good and worthy servant.

That being said, I've always had a hard time with the term, servant, which seems to imply to me the oppression of a task. Intellectually, I understand that the oppression of a task is the thought I bring to it, not necessarily the way it is. It's a choice of mind over matter. I believe that I understood in my call to ministry, I would essentially be a servant to many. I was energized by that thought, even though realizing that sometimes the servant would be torn between the act of servitude and become a burden.

The difference here, of course, is the attitude I bring to the act of service. I can do it graciously, or reluctantly which could make it a burden. However, choosing to walk the line of servanthood allowed me to be available to others without the fear of being a burden. To that end, I continue to strive within, of course, the parameters of my current limitations.

USEFUL

My life has always had to be useful, concurrent of course, with not wanting to be a burden. I suppose the notion that 'idol hands are tools of the devil,' which I often heard from the church growing up, has some dominion over my psyche. Granted, I don't believe in a 'devil' anymore, but the notion still has metaphorical merit. On the other hand, there was a positive take on that notion that we are to be Christ's servants in the world. I've always found my usefulness in Micah 6:8, NIV, *"What does the lord require of you but to serve justice, love mercy and walk humbly with your God."*

However, today I see it more through the eyes of the Zen Buddhist tradition, that we are to be mindful of each moment because each moment has its own usefulness. As hokey as it sounds, I believe that I must always be conscious of and serve the greater good. The problem, of course, is determining what the greater good is, and is my perspective on it really about the greater good, or simply my own personal desires? I would hope that they would be paired together. I know sometimes they are, other times, not so much. My life is often weaving in and out of what my eternal purpose is and my ego need.

Growing up, 'ego need' was called sin, falling short of God's purpose. I have always appreciated Dr. Wayne Dyer's acronym for sin: "Self-Inflicted Nonsense." That seems to say, for me, that I am often my own worst enemy. Certainly, as I have aged and have lost my physical ability to do certain things that I used to take for granted, in a phrase, it really pisses me off! My daily prayer consists of trying to accept and live within the parameters of my limitations, with patience! The patience part is sometimes more difficult than the limitation itself. However, each new day I have the opportunity to practice over again, limitation and patience! Grace does abound!

GRATITUDE

I Thessalonians 5:18, NIV says, "Give thanks in all circumstances…" if ever there was a year for that to be so, 2020 certainly fits the bill.

I try to live my life in gratitude. Notice, I said I try. Gratitude is important to me. Personally, I feel that I owe a great debt to all the people I have met and had the pleasure to learn from their tutelage; that also includes my nuclear and extended family. I have always believed the eastern maxim, "When the student is ready, the teacher will appear." That has been so true in my life. Sometimes, they are only here for a short while, but the opportunity to know and learn from them is wonderfully designed.

I believe that the universe (God) gives us daily opportunities to be worthy caretakers of mother earth and all therein. I believe gratitude to be a purposeful response to that. It becomes an "attitude of gratitude," and in order to take up that mantle, we have to truly believe in intentional and purposeful thanksgiving. Hence, as Paul says in Thessalonians, "Give thanks in all circumstances." The 13th-century mystic, Meister Eckhart, is credited with saying, "If you have only one prayer to give, let it be of gratitude."

So, how do you find gratitude for a year like 2020? The pandemic has decimated the world; no one has escaped its wrath. Here in the US of A, we lead the world in active cases and COVID-19 deaths. Not something to be proud of! We can blame the Trump administration for not taking the virus seriously, but blame does little to deal with the issue. People are losing their homes, having food insecurity, and lack basic income for loss of jobs. Again, what is there to be thankful for? The bar to be thankful is very low.

I write this on the eve of Thanksgiving 2020. The one thing I know about this Thanksgiving, it cannot be about wishing for what we would like it to be, but it must be about what is. The reality is, we must find our sense of gratitude in what we have on this very day.

I can give you a myriad of reasons why I should find disdain with this Thanksgiving, most having to do with the quality of my physicality and my grief for what our country has become. However, in spite of that, I believe in the greater good, the possibilities of the impossible, the universal intention of love, peace, and justice. FOR ALL. It provides me with the creative beauty and purpose of this home we call earth.

Yes, I am hopeful. Hopeful because my heart sings a song of praise for all that has been in my life, for all that is and for all that will be. I am eternally grateful for what my life has been and the many teachers, friends, acquaintances, and family that have helped me walk my path on this journey of life. Each day, I surrender myself to the Divine Spirit of Truth that manifests itself in my being and encourages me to be all I can be.

So yes, I will be thankful, full of gratitude for my journey in 2020 despite a pandemic and despite a nation torn asunder. I choose to believe that even amidst this notion, our country will survive, the pandemic will eventually be controlled, and we will be free to converse face to face again and share a mutual hug. For reasons of staying at home and safety, I can wait for that. Until that day, I will be grateful, and I bid you the same.

SPIRITUALITY

I have always had difficulty trying to be a 'religious' person. If you were to ask me today if I am religious, I would say no, I'm not particularly religious; however, I consider myself very spiritual. Religion is a construct of man's attempt to define God. It's consumed with dogma and ritual, and more often than not, one's religious experience is defined by dogma and ritual. The Sikh master, Kirpal Singh, says it this way, *"Religions have now been reduced to the mere performances like fasts and pilgrimages; wearing of particular apparel; white, yellow, blue, flame-colored or ochre robes; keeping peculiar marks on the body like tuft of hair on the head, sacred thread across the shoulder, circumcision or the five Kakas*; all of which have no substantial bearing, however remote, on the advancement of the soul towards self-realization and God realization." (Pg. 56, 'Spirituality, What it is,' Kirpal Singh, 1981 Ruhani Satsang.)*

* The Five Ks (Punjabi: ਪੰਜ ਕਕਾਰ *Pañj Kakār*) are five items that Guru Gobind Singh commanded Khalsa Sikhs to wear at all times in 1699. They are Kesh (uncut hair), Kangha (a wooden comb for the hair), Kara (an iron bracelet), Kachera (a 100% cotton tieable undergarment, must not be elastic), and Kirpan (an iron dagger large enough to defend oneself).

This is not to say that religion cannot convey a spiritual experience. I simply mean that the dynamic of dogma and ritual didn't do much for me.

I grew up in the Christian tradition, and that is my home base. I believe strongly in the teachings of Rabbi Jesus and that they lay a groundwork for a unique and grounded experience with the Divine. However, at this stage in my life, I don't believe that Jesus is the only way to the Divine. I believe that God has given us many paths to find him/her/it. I have spent time with the Buddhist Sangha and resonate with the teachings of the Buddha. I'm drawn to Chinese philosophy through Taoism (pronounced Dowism), the teachings of Lao-Tzu, and also find great solace in the Muslim mystic, Rumi. The upside of all of this is that once you seek and understand the principle of these traditions, at their core, they are basically the same. The golden rule seems to pervade their basic essence, and that love is the basic teaching. **
Each religious tradition, of course, have their own ritual and to some degree, dogma. It seems there are as many kinds of Buddhists as there are Baptists! However, the result is that we must pay our money and make a choice on the one that seems to best suit our spiritual needs. You may have to experience some different traditions to find the one that best resonates with your soul journey. Or, as Forrest Gump might say, "You have to go through a whole box of chocolates to find the one you really like." You might do as I do and integrate them all into your

own personal philosophy. That's okay; just know that there is a pathway for you.

Today, I am extremely comfortable in my skin. It is okay that folks can be whatever they want to be, worship however they choose to worship, and honor their God however they choose to do so. I will give them that respect. The moment they try and tell me my path is wrong, we will agree to disagree. I don't have a need that everyone should think and believe as I do. My journey is simply my journey and has nothing to do with you, just as your journey has nothing to do with me. Yet, I honor it and hope it serves you well.

At the core of all traditions is the basic notion of oneness. We all share the same DNA, brothers and sisters of creation. The uniqueness of creation is its variety, diversity, vitality, and sometimes leap to the unusual. Nothing surprises me anymore about this uniqueness, yet its constant beauty continues to stir my soul!

There is the tree, but there are thousands of different kinds of trees that take different shapes, big, tall, short, and small, some with fruits, others with seed pods, and many with just leaves. Millions of different kinds of flowers that share their effervescent scent amidst an array of color that is overwhelming. Birds, insects, animals all different and unique, and even humanity has its variety and diversity. There is only one race of men/women— the human race. Our culture would conclude that there are five or more different human races based on color and geography. Color has nothing to do with who we are as a human race. Color defines the uniqueness of creation only and is part of the rainbow of humanity's beauty of oneness.

The same can be said of sexual orientation. Cultural morality would have us believe that what has been labeled as homosexuality is an abasement to the creator, even though it has been practiced since man's inception. It is also found in the animal kingdom. I believe that gender preference is not a choice but a gift given at creation. Love knows no bounds and cannot be distinguished between sexual identities. Love is not male or female but simply divine.

So, what is my spiritual destination? Generally speaking, the role of our spirituality is to achieve enlightenment and/or salvation. I am not sure that is possible in only one lifetime, at least in my case. I believe in reincarnation that we have had many previous lives, each one moving us closer to enlightenment. The evidence for reincarnation is overwhelming by the example of creation itself and via the teaching of the sacred scriptures of most traditions. Some scholars believe that Christianity held the notion of reincarnation up until the 6th century. I have been told by at least three Intuitives that I was a pope in a previous incarnation. Unfortunately, not a good one!

Creation, nature, expresses itself through life, death, and resurrection. Each fall, the flowers die back into the ground, many trees lose their leaves and go dormant for the winter only to come back to life in the spring, sprouting new buds and leaves. Likewise, flowers remerge from their sacred death in the ground. Such is the natural order of things.

Many faith traditions teach the immortality of the soul. We are souls that have been given a body to work out our karma in a given lifetime. Our journey is basically the journey of the soul, winding its way through the vestiges of a lifetime, hoping the body will come along peacefully. However, it might not come along peacefully because of free-will. Enlightenment requires us to override the ego desires of the flesh and follow a path of love and righteousness, or what I interpret as *right-thinking*. This is simple in explanation but difficult in execution. However, that is the significance of the journey.

I wished that I could claim that I have mastered the 'soul perfection' of my journey. However, like the Apostle Paul says in his letter to the Romans 7:14, NIV ff, "We know that the law is spiritual; but I am unspiritual, sold as a slave to sin. I do not understand what I do. For what I want to do, I do not do, but what I hate I do. And if I do what I do not want to do, I agree that the law is good. As it is, it is no longer I myself who do it, but it is a sin living in me. For I know that good itself does not dwell in me, that is, in my sinful nature.[a] For I have the desire to do what is good, but I cannot carry it out. For I do not do the good I want to do, but the evil I do not want to do—this I keep on doing. Now, if I do what I do not want to do, it is no longer I who do it, but it is a sin living in me that does it."

Now, unlike Paul, I do not believe that I was born into sin or sold as a slave to sin. We can thank St. Augustine for developing the notion of original sin. I don't believe creation was done so in sin, let alone, God would intentionally create humanity with a negative stigma. Creation is bursting with positivity and perfection. A God of pure Love cannot create anything outside of love. It would be a contradiction of purpose and intention. Yet, as Paul claims, I sometimes do the things I don't want to do and don't do the things I know I should do, and that's what allows me to start fresh every morning, *"This is the day the Lord has made, I will rejoice and be glad in it." Psalm 118:24, NIV.*

To that end, I remain I am,
Curt

*Back in the fifties, you could buy formaldehyde across the pharmacy counter.

**(See the section on The Kingdom of God Within for a listing of the various faith traditions on the golden rule.)

THOUGHTS TO PONDER...

"God is not the exclusive property of any one tradition. The Divine light [cannot] be confined to a single lamp, belonging to the East or the West. But enlightens all human beings." - Karen Armstrong

In closing, let me reiterate the point that Jesus implied. He said, "I have come not to destroy the law but to fulfill it." Likewise, I write not to destroy the faith but to make it more understandable, more personal, and free from the chains of dogma.

The story of Christianity, as I have indicated in my writings, abounds with legend and myth. Its history is ragged and troublesome. The Crusades tried to mutilate the Muslims; "Kill a Muslim for Christ" was the battle cry. The idea of killing anyone in the name of Christ goes beyond my ability to understand it. In my thinking, it defies the very nature of my faith in God.

If your religion or faith tells you to kill someone in the name of your messenger, you have crossed the line of belief in Spirit and Love into a belief that "might is right and my God is stronger than your God." Physical, brute strength proves nothing other than that you are stronger than me. It has nothing to do with how either of us manifests the beliefs of our faith.

As I have matured in age, I have also matured in how I understand Christ and his message. The above essays are my attempt to show that understanding. I realize it may not do it for you. That's okay; I encourage you to take your own journey and look at the history of Christianity and the rise and fall of the faith. You may well be surprised at what you discover or not.

I am a seeker of truth and continue to be a student of "because I want to know." I understand that my ability to know is causally related to my ability to wrap my head around ideas I don't yet understand. It has nothing to do with whether I believe them or not. I want to know how they are connected, and how they relate to my present understanding of the faith, and the larger picture of Spirituality, which could change, if the ideas have merit and give me "goosebumps, or not!

If you have been able to work your way through all the Essays, without an OMG, I commend you. For those of you who think I have gone off the deep end as a heretic, I send blessings and gratitude for hanging in there. Though I would appreciate your honest feedback, you need to know that I have no investment in what you think about my writings. They are mine; I claim them, stand by them, and honor them because they come from deep inside me. They come from the core of my being and represent my truth. In the words of Martin Luther when he went before the Bishop's council, "Here I stand!"

Curt, 2021

BIBLIOGRAPHY

Bible quotations from: New International, and King James Version, except where noted.

'Abudu'l-baha, *Some Answered Questions*, National Spiritual Assembly of Baha'is in USA, 1930

Alexander, Eben, *Proof of Heaven*, Simon and Schuster Paperbacks, 2012

Borg, Marcus, The Heart of Christianity: Rediscovering a Life of Faith, Barnes & Noble, 2003

Borg, Marcus, *Jesus and Buddha*, Ulysses Press, 1997

Borg, Marcus, Crossan, John Dominic, *The Last Week*, Harper Collins, 2006

Borg, Marcus, Crossan, John Dominic, *The First Christmas*, Harper One, 2006

Braza, Jerry, *Seeds of Love*, Tuttle Publishing, 2011

Burton, Max, *Who Wrote the New Testament?* Harper Collins, 1989

Cannon, Dolores, *Jesus and the Essences*, Ozark Mountain Publications, 1992

Chopra, Deepak, *The Third Jesus*, Harmony Books, 2008

Davies, Stephan, *The Gospel of Thomas*, Skylight Paths Publishing, 2002

Dooley, Mike, *Life on Earth*, Hay House, 2016

Dyer, Wayne, *Wisdom of the Ages*, Harper Collins, 1998

Dyer, Wayne, *Living the Wisdom of the Tao*, 2008, Hay House Publishing, 2008

Eckhart, Meister, *Meister Eckhart* (Oliver Davis Translator), Penguin Books, 1994

Rocco Errico, *Aramaic Light on the Gospel of John*, Noohra Foundation, 2002

Rocco Errico, *Aramaic Light on the Gospel of Matthew*, Noohra Foundation, 2000

Ferrini, Paul, *Reflections of the Christ Mind*, Double Day Books, (Random House), 2000

Fox, Matthew, *The Tao of Thomas Aquinas*, IUniverse, 2020

Gottwald, Norman, *A Light to the Nations*, Harper, 1959

Greeley, Andrew, *Jesus, Meditations, and Stories...* Tom Doherty Associates, LLC, 2007

Hahn, Thick Nhat, *Living Buddha, Living Christ*, International Religious Foundation, World Scripture, Paragon House Riverhead Books, 1991

Hooper, Richard-Editor, Jesus, Buddha, Krishna, and Lao Tzu, The Parallel Sayings, Hampton Roads Publishing, 2007

Interlinear Greek-English New Testament, The, The Rev. Alfred Marshall, D. Litt., (translator) Samuel Bagster and Sons Limited, 1967

International Religious Foundation, *World Scripture*, Paragon House, 1991

Johnson, Julian, *The Path of the Masters*, Indraprastha Press (CBT), 1939

Lample, Paul, (Compiler), *Baha'u'llah's Teachings of Spiritual Reality*, Palabra Publications, 1996

Leong, Kenneth, *The Zen Teachings of Jesus*, Crossroads Publishers, 1995

McKiel, Allen, Beyond Tolerance, Interfaith Resources, 2007

McKiel, Allen, Human BeIng, Self-Publication, 2018

Mckiel, Allen, *Science, and Religion in the West*, Amazon, 2021

Notovich, Nicolas, The Unknown Life of Jesus Christ, Wilder Publications, 2008 edition

Prophet, Elizabeth Clare, *The Lost Teachings of Jesus*, Summit University Press, 1986

Schmidt, Daryl, *The Gospel of Mark*, Polebridge Press, 1990

Scott, Bernard Brandon, *Re-Imagining the World*, Polebridge Press, 2001

Singh, Kirpal, *Spirituality*, Ruhani Satsang, 1959

Spong, John Shelby, *A New Christianity for a New World*, Harper Collins, 2001

Spong, John Shelby, *Eternal Life*, Harper Collins, 2009

Spong, John Shelby, *Liberating the Gospels*, Harper Collins, 1996

Tillich, Paul, *The Dynamics of Faith*, Harper, and Row Publisher, 1957

Tillich, Paul, *The Shaking of the Foundations*, Charles Scribner and Sons, 1948

Walsh, Neal Donald, *Conversations with God, Vol. 1*, Putman and Sons, 1996

Walsh, Neal Donald, *What God Said*, The Berkeley Publishing Group, 2013

Weiss, Johannes, *The History of Primitive Christianity, Vol. 1,2*, Wilson-Erikson Incorp., 1937

Yogananda, Paramahansa, *Autobiography of a Yogi*, Self-Realization Fellowship, 1946

Yogananda, Paramahansa, *The Second Coming of Christ*, Self-Realization Fellowship, 2004

Yogananda, Parmanhansa, *The Yoga of Jesus*, Self-Realization Fellowship, 2007

Printed in the United States
by Baker & Taylor Publisher Services